THE MYTH MAKERS

THE
MYTH MAKERS

Literary Essays

———◆———

V.S. Pritchett

VINTAGE BOOKS
A Division of Random House • New York

Library of Congress Cataloging in Publication Data
Pritchett, Victor Sawdon, Sir, 1900–
The myth makers.
Bibliography: p.
1. Literature, Modern—19th century—History and
criticism—Addresses, essays, lectures. 2. Literature,
Modern—20th century—History and criticism—
Addresses, essays, lectures. I. Title.
[PN761.P7 1981]   809   80-6143
ISBN 0-394-74682-1 (pbk.)

Manufactured in the United States of America

FOR MY WIFE

Contents

PASTERNAK

Unsafe Conduct

THE SUPPRESSION OF *Dr Zhivago* in 1957 exposed the obsequious proceedings of the Union of Soviet Writers to international ridicule and contempt. We know now that after publishing a portion of autobiography, *Safe Conduct*, in 1931, Pasternak had published no original work under the Stalinist repression between 1932 and 1943 and that he was silenced by the absurd gauleiter Zhdanov from 1946 to 1954. Cautiously Pasternak planned a collection of poems to introduce an *Essay in Autobiography*, his natural mode, which would have prepared the way for a fuller understanding of the novelist's idiosyncrasy and imagination, and the changes they passed through since *Safe Conduct* was written.

The *Essay* was translated by Manya Harari in 1959. It is short enough to give some idea, Pasternak says, 'of how in my individual case, life became converted into art and art was born of life and experience'. It is a reminiscence touched upon tactfully and confined within the narrator's intimate circle. To take the story further and describe a 'world, unique and not to be compared with any other', a writer would have to write 'in such a way as to make the hair rise and the heart falter'. So the book is a reticent sketch, but does draw at least an outline. As Edward Crankshaw says in his warm introduction, Pasternak's battle has been with himself. Is there any other battle for an artist? His achievement is to have upheld the fact of the artist's conscience in a time when committees, programme makers, administrators and so on, thought literature had obligations to *them*! 'I dislike my style before 1940,' Pasternak says, 'just as I quarrel with half of Mayakovsky's writing and some of Yesenin's. I dislike the disintegrating forms, the impoverished thought and the littered, uneven language of those days. It is more important in life to lose than to acquire. Unless the seed dies it bears no fruit.' *Safe Conduct*—the earlier autobiography—dies: *Dr Zhivago* is born. *Safe Conduct* is a congested poetic embryo.

Part of Pasternak's tenacity comes from his upbringing and an inherited, strong yet evasive gaiety of spirit. The *Essay* sketches a family and circle of like-minded friends dedicated to the arts. The father, a painter, was a friend of Tolstoy; the mother, a distinguished pianist. Scriabin came to the house and the young Pasternak decided to become a composer and pianist. The portraits are less reminiscent than active, for Pasternak's prose, even in translation, has the present clarity of notes struck on the keys of a piano. The preoccupation with the ideas of resurrection and rebirth must have, I think, a link with the re-creating effect of music which never embalms a past. Scriabin and the elder Pasternak went for walks:

> Scriabin liked to take a run and then go on skipping along the road like a stone skimming the water, as if at any moment, he might leave the ground and glide on air. In general, he had trained himself in various kinds of sublime lightness and un-burdened movement verging on flight.

He defended Nietzsche, and we find in Pasternak's comment the traditional Russian feeling for the limitless. It was also Dostoevsky's:

> Scriabin's defence of the superman was an expression of his native Russian craving for the superlative. Indeed, it is not only true that music needs to be more than itself if it is to mean any-thing, but that everything in the world must surpass itself in order to be itself. There must be something limitless in a human being and in his activity for either to have definition and char-acter.

The elder Pasternak had to make a drawing of Tolstoy on his deathbed at the station of Astapovo; the son went with him. In the corner of the room lay

> a wrinkled old man, one of the dozens of old men invented by Tolstoy and scattered through his books. The place bristled with fir saplings which stood round the bed, their outlines sharpened by the setting sun. Four slanting sheaves of light reached across the room and threw over the corner where the body lay the sign of the big shadow of the crosspiece of the window and the small childish crosses of the shadows of the firs.

Outside the World Press 'brayed' and waiters at the station restaurant were galloping about with plates of 'underdone beef steaks. Beer flowed like a river'. The word 'underdone' evokes the whole of journalism in one of its raw and macabre news-gathering fiestas.

Pasternak gave up music because he found he lacked perfect pitch. He was sent to Germany for his education, travelled to Venice. He was the equipped intellectual. He felt the excitement of that iconoclasm which was to provoke the last glories of art in Europe. The poets Mayakovsky, Yesenin, Marina Tsvetayeva and Paolo Yashili come in. There is excitement and argument and then the aftermath; the tragic list of suicides—Mayakovsky killing himself (out of pride); Yesenin (without thinking it out) carelessly; Marina Tsvetayeva because she could not put her work between herself and the reality of daily life any longer; Yashili bewitched by the purges. There is compassion for the wretched Fadaev, the novelist who sold out:

> And it seems to me that Fadaev, still with the apologetic smile which had somehow stayed with him through all the crafty ins and outs of politics, told himself just before he pulled the trigger: 'Well, now it's all over. Good-bye, Sasha'.

Fadaev once told me that the decline in the drawing of grotesque characters in the Soviet novel was due to the fact that, under Communism, people were better integrated!

To go back 28 years to *Safe Conduct* is to meet the affected Pasternak. His self-criticism is just. Edited by Stefan Schimanski, it was first published abroad in 1945 and has been reissued with an introduction by J. M. Cohen. The translation is by Beatrice Scott. Robert Payne has done the stories, which include *Aerial Ways* and *The Childhood of Luvers*. Mr Cohen translates the poems. Another version of *Safe Conduct*, the stories and poems, comes from Alec Brown and Lydia Pasternak-Slater. I prefer the Beatrice Scott translation: Mr Alec Brown is heroically literal when dealing with the images, but he is conventional and commonplace in the straightforward writing. It is not surprising that translators differ and that they should drop sentences in the dazzle they have to face. Here are two versions of the firework scene in Venice. From Beatrice Scott:

> Under the open sky the faces of the audience glowed with a clarity which is characteristic of the baths, as in a covered won-derfully illuminated hall. Suddenly from the ceiling of this imaginary ballroom fell a slight shower. But hardly had it begun when the rain ceased. The reflection of the illuminations simmered above the square in a coloured dimness. The bell tower of St Mark's cut like a red marble rocket into the rose mist in wreaths halfway up to its summit. A little farther off dark-olive steams circled, and as in a fairy tale the five-headed shell of the Cathedral hid within them.

Mr Alec Brown's version is rhetorical. It begins:

> The outdoor audience was drenched in a bathhouse froth of brilliance, as if in a magnificently illuminated ballroom. All at once a fictitious ceiling began gently sprinkling it as if the assembled audience were a seminal square of the far north. Scarcely had a shower of another sort begun than it suddenly ceased.

In what way can a square be seminal? Mr Brown has 'whorls of dark purple vapour' for Miss Scott's 'dark olive steams'. Miss Scott's renderings of Pasternak's reflections on the fertilizing conflicts in European culture are far clearer than Mr Brown's and the two translators have a serious difference of meaning in the passage on the roles of the genius, iconoclast and rebel. In Pasternak, the stress on tradition is strong; without it, he says, the rebellious are 'empty-handed'.

Safe Conduct is a longer, richer, denser autobiographical work than the *Essay* is. It contains a throbbing account of the poet's relationship with Mayakovsky and of the wild scene of grief at his death. Simplicity and the sense of the limitless favour the Russians in the expression of extreme emotions. The Western reader toils to impose order as he reads. One sees this again in the story of Pasternak's short love duel with his pretty cousin in Marburg in his student days. Each moment of this experience— and of all others—is so sensuously active that we have the characteristic Pasternak vision of chaotic sense impressions, all spring and the effervescence of the blood, yet enclosed as by a serene medallion. The affectations of style and the teasing out of the thought have their difficulty, which is a torture for translators who cannot catch the tone of a poet whose mind has been formed by music and, to some extent, by painting. One has one's doubts, in prose at any rate, about the value of putting one art to the service of another. In the story *Childhood of Luvers*, the beauty of the tale and the deep perception into a girl's life take time to emerge from the orchestration.

Pasternak never looks from society to the individual. Society is some formless thing, a general fate or flux of circumstance which, in his lifetime, has been riven by events that are like inexplicable storms and lightning—a symphony of which he does not know the score, but he does know that it cannot exist without him. Only, much later on, in the far future, will it be possible to understand what happened and what the symphony was.

There, once more, is the traditional Russian nostalgia for the future. It is a faith in distance. Pasternak is not a closed and accomplished egoist. His feeling for the autobiographical comes from a capacity for living and re-living and putting passion into it. His continual reflections on memory are those of one who thinks of memory not as a fixed picture, but as a force in motion, perhaps like a storm that has passed, but is still banked up and reverberating. The present has its *élan* because it is always on the edge of the unknown and one misunderstands the past unless one remembers that this unknown was once part of its nature. For this reason Pasternak is able to raid the past and carry off people and places from it with the gleam of their own passion and bewilderment still on them. Such a view of life is poetic in the absolute sense. It is as hostile to the academic attitude to literature—Pushkin's feelings for his wife are more important than Pushkinism—as it is to the -isms of religion, politics, history and economics. It is the role of the poet to look at what is happening in the world and to know that quite other things are happening.

Those who expect some kind of counter-revolutionary or anti-Soviet journalism from *Dr Zhivago* will be disappointed. It is not, in that sense, a political novel at all, although it is entirely about the effects of the revolution of 1905, the first world war, the 1917 revolution and the last war, upon a group of families of the upper-class intelligentsia and others. Pasternak is a-political. His temper is Christian; Marxism is dismissed scornfully as half-baked folly and pomposity. The ground is cleared for an account of what really happens to people in catastrophe and the human, moral and spiritual loss. Pasternak has written a confession of anguish. We see it largely in the experiences of Dr Zhivago, a young doctor and poet who is neither for nor against the regime, but who suffers and endures. The son of an alcoholic, wild millionaire whose suicide is un-forgettably described in the opening chapter, Zhivago is a man torn in half by events. He survives for a long time partly because he is a doctor. He sympathises with the revolutionary desire for social justice but many of his friends are on the White rather than the Red side. His chief idea is to save his wife and family and to get away from Moscow to some peaceful spot. He gets them, after an appalling journey, to Siberia. He is separated from them when he is taken prisoner by Partisans who need a doctor, although he frankly tells them he is not of their party. When he escapes he finds his wife has got away to Paris. He is starving and pursued but—cool, indecisive, numbed in heart by suffering—he makes no attempt to join her; neither, at the end of his long and moving love-affair with a woman called Lara— whom we have met earlier as a seduced schoolgirl—does he stick to her and save himself. Wrecked in health and demoralized, he goes to pieces in Moscow, marries a peasant girl, deserts her and dies, eventually, of a heart attack while trying to open the window of a Moscow tram. He is the complete Soviet non-hero; yet at his death, his poems and diaries are treasured by the young generation. They recognize the integrity of the irre-claimable citizen who has only a grudging respect for the Soviet system.

As a novelist's just interpretation of the rights and wrongs of history and revolution, *Dr Zhivago* is useless. A political critic would say that it wilfully left out half the drama and argument. Pasternak would agree. He would add that people who are living history cannot know what history really is. Dr Zhivago himself is a passive and truthful character—a man out of E. M. Forster—and he survives, as long as he does, by submission to fate. This is a strength because he is inflexible in the sense of vocation. He reminds one of Chekhov.

The temper of Zhivago's mind can be judged best in a few passages. Back from the Front in the first world war and seeing the revolution, he finds his upper-class friends colourless:

The fooling, the right of idleness enjoyed by the few while the majority suffered, could itself create an illusion of genuine character and originality.

But how quickly, once the lower classes and the rich had lost their privileges, how these people faded! How effortlessly they had given up the habit of independent thought—which at this rate could never in fact have been genuinely theirs!

On the leap from peace to 'mass insanity and to the savagery of daily, hourly, legalized, rewarded slaughter', Zhivago says:

> It was then that falsehood came to our Russian land. The great misfortune, the root of all the evil to come, was the loss of faith in the value of personal opinions. People imagined that it was out of date to follow their moral sense, that they must all sing in chorus, and live by other people's notions, the notions that were being crammed down everybody's throat. And there arose the power of the glittering phrase, first tsarist and then revolutionary. . . . Instead of being natural and spontaneous as we had always been we began to be idiotically pompous with each other.

He is sick of 'claptrap in praise of the revolution and the regime'. He can't accept that 'they' are all radiant heroes and he 'a mean little fellow'. A brilliant diagnostician, he is interested in mimesis in organisms. He gives a lecture, and there is a party outcry against his 'idealism, mysticism, neo-Schellingism'. The vulgarity of it disgusts him. Antipov—the husband of Lara, Zhivago's mistress—is a commissar whose star is beginning to fade. He is infected by obsessive self-criticism and the desire to confess:

> It was the disease, the revolutionary madness of the age; that in his heart everyone was utterly different from his words and the outward appearance he assumed. No-one had a clear conscience. Everyone had some reason to feel that he was guilty of every-thing, that he was an impostor, an undetected criminal. The

slightest pretext was enough to launch an orgy of self-torture. People slandered and accused themselves, not only out of terror but of their own will, from a morbidly destructive impulse, in a state of metaphysical trance, carried away by that passion for self-condemnation, which cannot be checked once it has been given free rein.

Zhivago's perennial longing is to get away from the emptiness and dullness of human verbosity and to take refuge in nature, in sleep, in grinding labour or understanding 'rendered speechless by emotion'.

But Zhivago's musings are a small part of a book which has countless precise pictures of revolutionary happenings, as they appeared to the private eye of the characters. Some, like the young Zhivago, the young Lara, the young Pasha, the young Tonya, have grown up in quiet intellectual circles; but there are the railway workers, the peasants, individuals taken out of the Russian mass and soon to be scattered, martyrized or transformed. In twenty-odd years they became unrecognizable to one another. The shy Pasha will become the truculent commissar; Lara, the sensual, tormented girl who was seduced while still at school, will become the austere hospital nurse, the difficult wife and—after her sufferings—the tragic mistress. Fatal separations come sooner or later to all and destroy the heart.

From the point of realism, Pasternak's use of far-fetched co-incidence to bring about meetings with his characters is absurd; but this book is really a romance in which the novelist is seeking the lineament or texture of a fate, not the detail of adventure or a construct of event and character. He jumps, without explanation, to new places and situations. How does Zhivago escape arrest after his unpopular lecture? How does he get to his hiding place in the forest? How did he intrigue? What happens to Lara when she is torn from Zhivago and goes off to degradation in China? These things are left out or are slurred over. The very slurring adds to our sense of the immeasurable quality of the general disaster. He conveys that cataclysms observably remove *meaning* from people's lives without leaving them futile.

Several large episodes stand out in the book, especially the long, quiet and unforgettable account of the Zhivago family's journey of escape by cattle-truck to Siberia. It takes them into the heart of the civil war, and yet (by a freak of war) into a village which is little touched by it and still living the old life. There are small episodes like the grotesque death of the revolutionary soldier Gintz who slips into a water-butt when he is making a speech. Simply because this happens suddenly and he looks so silly, a Cossack shoots him. Pasternak has an eye for the gratuitous actions of life; it deceives both in its fears and assurances. When the street fighting breaks out in Moscow, the Zhivago family is far more preoccupied with a fanatical attempt to make their stove work. Their child gets a sore throat and temperature and the guests they are sheltering bore them with ceaseless chatter. That is how revolution comes. Everywhere people are carrying their core of private life about with them. There is no cliché of invention in Pasternak; there is no eccentricity either. He has the eye of nature. Another refreshing quality is the freedom from the Anglo–American obsession with sex. In love, he is concerned with the heart. It is hard to imagine an English, French or American novel on Pasternak's subject, that would not be an orgy of rape or creeping sexuality.

Dr Zhivago is a great mound of minutely observed particulars and this particularity is, of course, expressive of his central attitude—his stand for private life and integrity. Even the look of the newspaper in which Zhivago reads the first news of the revolution is described. He stands reading, overwhelmed, in the snow which 'covered the pages with a grey, rustling, snowy gruel'. There is a similar instantaneous detail in the lovely observations of nature. The snow melts, the forest comes to life in the smoking and steaming months of the thaw.

Ancient pine trees, perched on dizzy heights, drank moisture almost from the clouds and it foamed and dried a rusty white at their roots like beer-foam on a moustache. The very sky, drunk with spring and giddy with its fumes, thickened with clouds. Low clouds, drooping at the edges like felt, sailed over the woods, and rain leapt from them, warm, smelling of soil and sweat, and washing the last of the armour-plating of ice from the earth.

Yury woke up, stretched, raised himself on one elbow and looked and listened.

At another point, in a vermin-infested house, he writes of the rats, flopping down and squealing in their 'disgusting, pitiful, contralto voices'.

Dr Zhivago might be called an autobiography which breaks the rules and turns novel, reckless of form and restrictions of point of view. Pasternak never resists any hour of life that can be crystallized and fixed for ever, even if it is a digression. But we can guess, from Dr Zhivago's notes and especially from one which defends the 'seemingly incongruous jumble of things and ideas in the work of the Symbolists against the charge of stylistic fancy', that Pasternak's writing lives in the instant. The chief characters appear and then dive out of sight into time. Moving, urgent, vivid, they are suddenly swept away into nothingness. Zhivago's mistress vanishes into the street, was probably arrested (he says) and died in some labour camp 'as so many people did in those days'.

This does not make them seem futile. Zhivago's demoralization has the effect of giving edge to his moral criticism. He is scornful when two of his friends, who are jailed and 're-educated', boast of their reformation: Dudorov taking the text-book orthodoxy of his sentiments as a sign of humanity. 'Men who are not free, he thought, idealize their bondage,' says Zhivago.

Health is ruined by the systemic duplicity forced on people if you say the opposite of what you feel, if you grovel before what you dislike and rejoice at what brings you nothing but misfortune. Your nervous system isn't a fiction, it's a fact of your physical body and your soul exists in space and is inside you like the teeth in your head. You can't keep isolating it with impunity. I found it painful to listen to you, Nicky, when you told how you were re-educated and grew up in jail. It was like listening to a circus horse describing how it broke itself in.

The doctor is the self-perfecting man and saint who goes down-hill as a citizen. He refuses to be neutered by mediocre optimism. His story marks the return to the compassion of the great Russian tradition and repudiates the long, long reign of highly-coloured journalism and neo-Victorianism in Soviet writing.

SOLZHENITSYN

The Gulag Circle

AS A NOVELIST Solzhenitsyn is very much in the powerful
tradition of the nineteenth-century Russian novel as it appears
in the prophet-preacher writings of Tolstoy and Dostoevsky,
now one, now the other; as a polemical writer, in the tradition
of Belinsky and Herzen. If history has altered his ground, another difference seems to me important. As far as one can judge
he is far removed from the influences Western genius had upon
his predecessors—for example, Shakespeare, Cervantes, Sterne,
Dickens—his indoctrination as a young Komsomol was political and scientific. It is true that he was a poet, had read the poets
of the revolutionary period and intended to be a novelist, but
the tendencies of his youth drew him to the documentary and
his unrest to a documentary which defied the Stalinist political
monopoly of this mainly 'useful' form of writing. Since he is a
passionate man, equipped with searing powers of irony, he was
certain to find that man does not live by the record alone, but
by the myths he creates, myths which contain his private
thoughts and that sense of being 'elsewhere' when dogma becomes despotic. From Tolstoy and Dostoevsky, and as a man
of imagination, he learned to hate contemporary materialism.
There is a passage in the last of the Gulag volumes which makes
the point:

> We don't mind having a fellow countryman called Lev Tol-
> stoy. It's a good trade-mark. (Even makes a good postage stamp.)
> Foreigners can be taken on trips to Yasnaya Polyana. . . . But
> my dear countryman, if someone takes Tolstoy seriously, if a
> real-life Tolstoyan springs up among us—hey, look out there!
> Mind you don't fall under our caterpillar tracks.

Not exactly the *style* of Tolstoy; it is closer to the crowd style of Dostoevsky.

Solzhenitsyn's reputation was made by the simple stark reporting of the horror and degradation of the labour camps, in *One Day in the Life of Ivan Denisovich*. The title phrase 'one day' is not only a clue to its immediacy, but far more to the tradition that the Russian novelists do not move by plot-time—which is an artifice—but by the felt hours of the day that run into each other. In its simplicity this 'story' is still the finest and most apprehensible thing he has written, for the prophet-preacher does not obtrude upon the simple character whose humble tale is told. He became a novelist in *Cancer Ward* and *First Circle*. Here documentary and the novel merge. The autobiographical element is strong but the symbols grow larger than the personal report of the author's own story. *Cancer Ward* is close to his own history. A twenty-six-year-old Captain of Artillery in East Prussia, with a university degree in mathematics and physics, he was sentenced to eight years of forced labour, for making derogatory remarks about Stalin. He was not freed until 1956. In exile in Kazakhstan where, in his time, Dostoevsky had also been sent—Solzhenitsyn was treated for a tumour and recovered. In this picaresque novel—the sick are the picaros of contemporary life—we get a day-by-day account of the life of an overcrowded cancer hospital, an exhaustive analysis of how cancer distorts the life stories of the patients and the doctors, and this is a way of describing what Russian life is really like outside. Hospital is like prison; it isolates. Every man and woman has his tale on his tongue; having cancer is a way of life. The people are all far from home, owing to the war or exile, and one sees the part played by distance, anarchy, and chance. The hospital is really an obscene Collective. Illness and overwork pretty well destroy private relationships; the irony is that the unanswerable punishments of Nature free one from the malice of the Secret Police and one has a brief liberty before one dies. The comedy is black: a philologist, for example, gets cancer of the larynx! No more languages for him. If you are a Party man, like the careerist Rusanov, you are astonished that your power has gone. His bed lies between the beds of two men condemned to exile:

> If Pavel Nikolayevich were the same man he had been before he entered hospital, he would have gone and raised the question as a matter of principle—how could they put executive officials among dubious, socially harmful elements? But in the five weeks that the tumour had pulled him about as if he were a fish on a hook, Pavel Nikolayevich had either mellowed or become a simpler man.

Rusanov is quietly drawn as a Iudushka or hypocrite—see Shchedrin's classic portrait of the Russian Judas in *The Golovlyov Family*—a tedious, self-complacent, and exacting bureaucrat: he thinks he has the right to be the first to read the Party newspaper when it is brought to the ward; he is a glutton for all the boring articles about economics and politics. At first illness terrifies him, but as he recovers, his arrogance returns. Still, he has been a little mellowed until a new fear arises from the news that a new Presidium has been elected and that an investigation of the delinquencies of Stalinism will take place. He is calmed by his awful go-getting daughter who has written a few poems and has just intrigued her way into the Union of Soviet Writers. She tells her father that he need not worry; its only a question of knowing the ropes and she has learned the tricks. He need not worry too much about that shameful intrigue by which he arranged to have someone sent to a labour camp in order to get the man's apartment.

The cancer ward is, of course, a symbol of Russia under Stalinism. The patients talk of their lives and their beliefs, and above all of the conflict between those who believe in power and those who rebelliously think of private happiness. Most accept the Communist society; it is daily life. But the experience of one or two has shown them what has been lost: the moral ideal of socialism. (The loss is like the loss of the American dream.) The ward is a sort of confessional. So far the limits of the novel are familiar; but halfway through there is a scene which shows Solzhenitsyn breaking new ground. He gives us that portrait of a happy family, the simple, ingenuous Kadims who, expecting nothing from the life of harsh exile, had found an absurd happiness with their dogs and cats: it recalls the idyllic pages of *Oblomov*. Solzhenitsyn is opening a window on a subject that has so far been obsessive and claustrophobic. In *First Circle*, he is quietly in command of powers that were scattered and now, like the great novelists, can control an orchestrated theme. The idea is taken from Dante. The first circle of Hell in Dante is the fate of the pre-Christian philosophers who are doomed to live there for eternity, and it is represented by the Mavrino Institute for scientific research on the outskirts of Moscow. The year is 1949, Stalin is ageing and becoming more ruthless. The Institute is staffed by scientists, engineers and academicians who have been taken out of the labour camps to do technical work under conditions only slightly less awful than the brutal conditions of the camps, for though they eat better, they are still cut off almost completely from their families. Most have been prisoners for ten years; at the end of it, their terms will probably be extended to twenty-five. They know they are there for eternity. With them, under the efficient police system, work a number of free workers from outside who go home at night and who act, together with some of the prisoners themselves, as informers. Eternal damnation could not be more certain. If their particular usefulness comes to an end, the prisoners will be returned to the savage camps and die at last in the prison hospital. It is exactly like the system applied to foreign workers by the Nazis during the war: feed them little, exhaust their muscles and brains, and let them die.

But eternal damnation is a kind of freedom, just as having cancer is. The prisoners of Mavrino have adapted themselves to their fate. Among them is the brilliantly drawn Rubin, a Jew and Party member, a philologist who was an organizer of sabotage in Germany during the war: then there are Nerzhin, a mathematician who has been a soldier; Pryanchikov, an engineer; Spiridon, a peasant and glass blower who has been taken on by mistake: Doronin, a young double agent: Sologdin, a designer, a recalcitrant in for a twenty-five year stretch. Their task is sinister: to design an apparatus for codifying speech patterns and tracing telephone calls—a machine that Stalin has specially asked for. It will lead to a huge increase in arrests and the novel indeed opens with a scene in which Innokenty Volodin, a diplomat, foolishly uses the telephone to warn a friend not to give a certain medicine to a foreign professor. By the end of the novel the completed apparatus traps him. It is typical of Solzhenitsyn that women play only a small part in the book. They are lost, touching, lonely figures and in only two or three chapters do they have any part. Incidentally, one characteristically Victorian aspect of the book is its scant interest in the perverting of sexual life in prison. Love is sorrow and sex is 'outside' and regarded as rather disgraceful. The idea owes something to Russian puritanism.

Within Solzhenitsyn's scheme, we see the curious nervous eagerness of life in prison, listen to the life stories, watch the effect of prison on character—on the guards and officials in charge. The prisoners are known as *zeks*:

. . . One of those age old prison arguments was in progress. When is it best to be imprisoned? The way the question was put presupposed that no one was ever destined to avoid prison. Prisoners were inclined to exaggerate the number of other prisoners. When, in fact, there were only 12 to 15 million human beings in captivity, the zeks believed there were 20 or even 30 million. They believed that hardly any males were still free. 'When is it best to be imprisoned?' simply meant was it better in one's youth or in one's declining years. Some zeks, usually the young ones, cheerfully insisted that it was better to be imprisoned in one's youth. Then one had a chance to learn what it meant to live, what really mattered and what was crap; then at the age of 35, having knocked off a ten year term, a man could build his life on intelligent foundations. A man who'd been imprisoned in old age could only suffer because he hadn't 'lived right', because his life had been a chain of mistakes, and because those mistakes could no longer be corrected. Others—usually these older men—would maintain no less optimistically that being imprisoned in old age is, on the contrary, like going on a modest pension into a monastery; one had already drawn everything from life in one's best years. (In a prisoner's vocabulary 'Everything' narrowed down to the possession of a female body, good clothes, good food and alcohol.) They went on to prove that in camp you couldn't take much hide off an old man, whereas you could wear down and cripple a young man, so that afterwards he 'wouldn't even want to get a woman'.

Rubin, the logical Jewish Communist, accepts prison, because 'the ways of Socialist truth are sometimes tortuous'. He has a violent row with Sologdin, the unrepentant designer, that goes to the heart of the novel. The row is about ends and means. An excellent distinction is made: Rubin's situation 'seemed to him tragic in the Aristotelian sense'. He had been

dealt a blow by the hands of those he loved the most (the Party). He had been imprisoned by unfeeling bureaucrats because he loved the common cause to an improper degree. As a result of that tragic contradiction, in order to defend his dignity and that of his comrades, Rubin found himself compelled to stand up daily against the prison officers and guards whose actions, according to his view of the world, were determined by a totally true, correct and progressive law.

The other zeks are against him and persecute him. The quarrels are wrecking the health of this clever, emotional man. Sologdin is his worst persecutor.

> Sologdin knew very well that Rubin was not an informer and would never be one. But at the moment the temptation was great to lump him with the security officers. . . .

Sologdin says:

> 'Since all of us have been imprisoned justly and you're the only exception, that means our jailers are in the right. Every year you write a petition asking for a pardon . . .'
> 'You lie! Not asking for a pardon, but for a review of my case.'
> 'What's the difference?'
> 'A very big difference indeed.'

As a Party member, though in disgrace, Rubin makes his Jesuitical point.

'They turn you down and you keep on begging,' Sologdin reports. And, Sologdin says, *he* would never demean himself, by begging. (And in fact, he doesn't: Sologdin is a student of human weakness. He shrewdly waits till he has a brilliant idea about the encoding device and boldly plays one prison official off against another in a feat of blackmail which is the only thing officials are frightened of.)

And now we see Solzhenitsyn's mastery as a novelist: he is able to see the consoling contradictions of human nature and how they fertilize character. Rubin is not only the subtle and passionate Jewish Marxist and 'sea-lawyer': he is also the born Jewish comedian: he entertains the prisoners with a farcical historical parody of their own trials, filled with faked evidence from poetry, prison slang and innuendoes. And there is even more to this richly sympathetic man. His successes make him miserable and he becomes the practical Jewish mystic who is working on a plan for ritualizing Communist life by introducing Civic Temples!

The density of Solzhenitsyn's texture owes everything to the ingenious interlocking of incidents that are really short stories. This is the form in which he excels. His philosophical and political debates are always in this lively and purposive story form. He never fails to move forward. And the stories build up the central idea. The later tendentious Tolstoy is an obvious influence, more marked than Dostoevsky's in *The House of the Dead*. Our eye is on the most tragic character: Nerzhin, and his concern with what a man must do with his life. It is through his sorrow that we see that, bad as the lot of the prisoners is, the lot of their wives whom they can scarcely ever see or write to is a worse imprisonment in the open. They dare not easily admit that their husbands are political prisoners, for they will be shunned. Guilt by association is like plague: one is unclean. Nerzhin is a genuine stoic—in contrast to the endangered diplomat Volodin who is a genuine epicurean. Both men know they are doomed. In his early days as a Communist Nerzhin had noticed that educated or 'liberal' prisoners always let him down in a crisis; he turned idealistically to 'the People' in the labour camps and found they were worse.

> It turned out that the People had no homespun superiority. . . . They were no more firm of spirit as they faced the stone walls of a ten-year term. They were no more far-sighted than he during the difficult moments of transport and body searches. They were blinder and more trusting about informers. They were more prone to believe the crude deception of the bosses. . . .

With great tact Nerzhin nevertheless cultivates the peasant Spiridon who feels tragically the separation from his family, because in the family he saw the only meaning to life. He can never argue or think much but hits the nail on the head, peasant-fashion, with a proverb. His eventual reply to the question 'How can anyone on earth really tell who is right and who is wrong? Who can be sure?' is devastating:

The wolfhound is right and the cannibal is wrong.

(Solzhenitsyn has read Hemingway and this scene reminds one of the only good thing in *For Whom the Bell Tolls*—the long talk with the Spanish peasant at the bridge in the Guadarrama.) Spiridon's view of life (Nerzhin sees) has an important and rare characteristic: it is his own. Nerzhin reflects:

> What was lacking in most of them (the People) was that personal *point of view* which becomes more precious than life itself.
>
> There was only one thing left for Nerzhin to do—to be himself . . . the People is not everyone who speaks our language, nor yet the elect marked by the fiery stamp of genius. Not by birth, not by the work of one's hands, not by the wings of education, is one elected into the people.
>
> But by one's inner self.
>
> Everyone forgets his inner self year after year. One must try to temper, to cut, to polish one's soul so as to become *a human being*.
>
> And thereby become a tiny particle of one's people.

Nerzhin's integrity detaches him from the others; on matters of regulation and principle he risks everything with the officials and guards and insists on straight or cold ironic confrontations. They fear his powers of irony. Naturally—and he knows it—he will be sent back to the labour camp. He has understood the awful words 'For ever' as few of the others have; the words mean 'You have exhausted your power to hurt me'.

A passionate and agonized book like Dostoevsky's *The House of the Dead* owes much to the Romantic belief in the supreme value of suffering which is often said to be fundamental among Slavs. Prison has the monastic lure. Many of Solzhenitsyn's characters are haunted by this acceptance, but there is nothing mystical or romantic in him. He is quite clear that the Mavrino is not the Chateau d'If or Gorky's Siberia, that something has gone morally wrong and that courage in a changed attitude to the self is the important thing. He is, as I have said, more Tolstoyan than Dostoevskian.

The novel is not a sprawling, flat panorama, in spite of its range of scenes inside and outside prison. It has a serene command of space and time. It has architectural unity, and once the uneasy opening chapters are over, it is unshakeable. This beginning does contain, in my opinion, one weakness: the novelist has, with a daring which I find merely journalistic, introduced a live portrait of the ageing Stalin alone in his rooms. I simply do not believe the following words:

> But reviewing in his mind the not-so-complex history of the world, Stalin knew that with time people would forgive everything bad, even forget it, even remember it as something good. Entire peoples were like Lady Anne, the widow in Shakespeare's *Richard III*. Their wrath was short-lived, their will not steadfast, their memory weak—they would always be glad to surrender themselves to the victor.

A word about Solzhenitsyn's style: in these novels it is close to the vernacular and spiced with slang and proverbs and in two respects resembles the plain style of Swift: it sways between savage, educated irony and the speech of the people. Solzhenitsyn delights in exposing official prose and its deceits. There are two passages in *First Circle* which comment on the 'popular' or 'newspaper' style used by the poets when they addressed 'the People'.

> Mayakovsky, for instance, considered it an honour to use a newspaper clipping as an epigraph for a poem. In other words he considered it an honour not to rise above the newspapers. But then why have literature at all?

For a good reason

a great writer—forgive me, perhaps I shouldn't say this, I'll lower my voice—a great writer is so to speak a second government, that's why no regime anywhere has ever loved its great writers only its minor ones.

Whether Solzhenitsyn still intends to complete the historical trilogy he began in *August 1914* and continued in the fragment *Lenin in Zurich* is not clear. The influence of the Tolstoy of *War and Peace* is explicit. The subject of *August 1914* is the invasion of East Prussia and the military disaster of Tannenberg and that is the perfect Tolstoyan subject. It contains all the ironies: a General Staff corrupted by court favouritism and more concerned with seniority than battle; a muddled and ill-prepared campaign; yet a defeat which nevertheless did draw off so many German troops from the West that it enabled the French to save Paris at the Marne. There were two rival and out-of-date plans of campaign; drive into East Prussia with overwhelming man-power, cut off the East Prussian salient at the shoulder and encircle it: or force the way through to Berlin. If we check Solzhenitsyn's account with what the military historians have said, we find he is completely accurate. The actions of General Samsonov, the commander of the second Russian army that was destroyed, are set out correctly; the fact that the sad general was the victim of rival generals and criminally ill-equipped and cut off from information, is set out in the history books, down to such details as the lack of wire for his field telephones and the neglect of signal codes, so that he had to send out all messages *en clair*.

The other figures in the High Command—Danilov, the master strategist, the Grand Duke Nicolas, Zhilinsky who cheated, the obsequious Yanushekevich who buried his incompetence in paper work—are drawn to the life and, at the end of the book, there is a searching account of their behaviour at the conference table when the white-washing of their responsibilities is completed. Solzhenitsyn has examined all the records. But until I read all this elsewhere I was often lost in his account of the confusion of the campaign: the great Tolstoy was a master of confusion in the field. He made the disposition of forces clear: one follows him easily without a map. To follow Solzhenitsyn without a map is very difficult. Still, in Vorotyntsev, the staff officer and fictional character who carries the moral burden of the narrative, we have the well-drawn portrait of both a feeling man and an intelligent professional soldier who can not only guide his remnant out of the mess, but who can guide us too.

Solzhenitsyn has Tolstoy's eye for the meaninglessness and the futilities of war—the town captured and then evacuated for no reason that is clear to the army; the loss of contact; the mystery of one's situation; the contradiction of orders; the jealousies of the officers; the baffled faces of the fatalistic troops; and when there is a question of action any given incident is vividly done and without journalistic rhetoric. One is struck, when Solzhenitsyn singles out an officer or a common soldier, by the fact that it is their particular type of mind that is thoroughly presented to us: they are thinking animals rather than the frightened, mad, simple, hysterical or violent men who appear in nearly all post-Tolstoyan books on war and in which war is turned into orgy. In the narrative the horror tends to be generalized, but here we notice an odd innovation. It seems that Solzhenitsyn either intended two kinds of war narrative, one to be read and the other to be filmed; or that a film director has inserted intervals of script-writing in which the physical horrors of war are set up for the exploiting cameraman. This insertion of film frankly destroys the illusion and if it is a new literary device it is a disaster and strikes one as cynical.

There are two exceptionally fine moments in the narrative. We have seen General Samsonov in all his moods but when the debâcle comes, he splits: half of him thinks he has an army still, the other wanders about with an innocent, mad smile on his face, raising his cap politely to his soldiers who themselves don't know whether they are soldiers any more. This and other passages are as good as anything in Vigny's *Servitude et grandeur militaires*. The other is a long episode describing the escape of Vorotyntsev and his remnant, through the forests and through the encircling German advance. They will succeed. We know from history what their lives are likely to become and by this hindsight it would have been easy for the author to show them with bitter irony as the marionettes of fate, but Solzhenitsyn rejects that; rather he speaks for them as the novelist should, feeling with the ignorance of each one in his different way and himself moving with their changes of feeling. This sensibility to change in the mind and heart is important to the book's intention, which is to show both the innocence and the ignorance of these men's involvement as they advance into their own and their country's future. He is clearly working up to a humane, sceptical exploratory conception of Russian history that will grow more and more at variance with official conclusions.

The war therefore is folly; when the son of one of the advanced families joins up patriotically he is regarded by his young friends as a traitor to an enlightened education. They are not part of the rootless intelligentsia; they are sincere, without being seriously deluded in their desire to get closer to the people. They, too, can't know their future and Solzhenitsyn has presented their innocence with the slow-moving care that he is to show in portraying the soldiers. One's picture of Russians of this kind in this period has been so stereotyped by Gorki and the melodramatic denigration of Marxists that one is astonished by the absence of the usual teeth-grinding doctrinal hatred and by the evidence of a free witness. Underlying the book is the criticism of the dogma that history can be rationally known or governed. History, says a teasing old professor to one of the ingenuous young students in the story, grows like a living tree.

Lenin in Zurich consists of a number of chapters which Solzhenitsyn cut out of *August 1914* because they ran too far ahead of the time scale of the huge historical chronicle he had in mind. These chapters have a natural intensity and unity, and something of the scenario for a film. We are plunged suddenly into Lenin's mind without preparation, as he stands with his wife and mother-in-law on an Austrian station platform staring at the engine of the train—frightening image of impersonal power—which will soon carry them to Cracow. The 1914 war has taken the logician by surprise. So deep in the tactics and mechanics of conspiracy is he that he simply has not expected the onset of a stupendous act of history and is utterly unprepared for its accidental element. Once more—as in 1905—the conspirator finds real life has outpaced the tactician. When the train gets to Cracow his situation has again changed; he will have to make for neutral Switzerland. But at Cracow, where the first Polish wounded are arriving and the crowds of women are weeping over the stretchers, he has already been revived by an exultation that will keep him going:

> Piss-poor, slobbering pseudo-socialists with the petit-bourgeois worm in them would try to capture the masses by jabbering away 'for peace'. They must be hit first and fast. Which of them has the vision to see and the strength of mind to embrace the great decision ahead: not to try and stop the war, but to step it up? To transfer it—*to your own country*.
>
> 'Peace' is a slogan for fatheads and traitors! What is the point of a hollow peace that nobody needs, unless you can convert it immediately into *civil war with no quarter given*?

In the next three years Solzhenitsyn puts us inside Lenin's mind, crushes us against it, entangles us with it, takes us down into the pit of his rancours, the frustrations and the hatred that sustain him, as he keeps the political machine in his mind oiled and free of rust, while he is forced to live in limbo.

The thing was to be immediate on shifting ground. The war was a gift in itself to revolutionaries, but now—where would the revolution start? Russia was inaccessible. The one idea the war made plausible was the idea of permanent revolution, i.e. permanent civil war. Why could it not begin in neutral Switzerland? The idea came to nothing: the 'swinish' Swiss socialists were pusillanimous. They were in love with 100 years of petit-bourgeois neutrality; and were more interested—how could you believe it!—in defending their country? This failure made him furious with himself; why hadn't he seen that Stockholm was the place to set the world revolution going? In the end, the Germans were plotting to use him against the Tsarists and he had the humiliation of hearing from others not condemned to inactivity (writing pamphlets in the Zurich library), and—in 1917—he was once more taken by surprise and did not for a long time believe that the Revolution had begun in Russia.

Of course, this is a gross simplification of Solzhenitsyn's chronicle. *That* depends on his plausible if hostile estimate of Lenin's introspections, as they torment his mind and become minutely argued decisions. Solzhenitsyn says that the dialogue in the book is documented and close to the dreary language of the dialectic in which Lenin and his conspirators habitually chatted. One can be sure of that, and it is a relief to come upon two scenes in which Lenin is brought to life by rogues, the fantastic Parvus, the millionaire conspirator and the brilliantly cynical Radek. This journalist is at his merriest when it comes to writing articles or letters of eager duplicity. The sight of shamelessness so happy and inspired is almost cheering. As for the fat Parvus who has made millions in Turkey and delights in getting funds for revolutionaries out of capitalist financiers—he is a sort of stage magician. He knows money is power and simply loves playing with it in order to buy women, chateaux and, in a most disinterested way, leaders. Thus he has been invaluable to the conspirators. The Red millionaire had no faith, we are told, in the Bolsheviks' organizing ability. He attacked Lenin's concessions to the peasants. He ended by building himself an opulent house on the island of Schwanenberger in Germany and lived there to enjoy his orgies for the rest of his life.

A Doctor

THE MARK OF genius is an incessant activity of mind. Genius is a spiritual greed. By the time of his death from tuberculosis when he was in his early forties, Chekhov had spent whatever breath he had, in every minute, not only in the writing of his hundreds of stories, his plays and his research on the convict island of Sakhalin—where he even took a census—but in exhausting work as a doctor, a founder of clinics and hospitals, schools and libraries, as the practical manager for many years of a small estate, as an indefatigable traveller in Russia, Europe and Asia.

From the age of nineteen he supported his family—a bankrupt despotic shop-keeping father, his fretful mother, a string of bickering relatives and hangers-on—mainly by his writing, under knockabout domestic conditions which were farcically at variance with what a serious artist is supposed to need. He appointed himself—even at nineteen—head of this tribe, who were 'depressed by the abnormality of living together' and who were people (he wrote in one of his letters) 'pasted together artificially'. They were touchy, lazy, talkative, noisy, pretentious and incurably hard up. Simply to listen to the noise they made drove him to despair and made him dizzy. To his brother he wrote—I quote from David Magarshack's *Anton Chekhov: A Life*:

You know that I have a whole multitude of grown-up people living under the same roof with me. Because of some inexplicable set of circumstances we don't find it possible to separate: mother; sister; Michael who won't leave till he has finished his university course; Nicholas who is doing nothing and who has been jilted by his lady love and is always drunk and walking about in rags; auntie and Alexey who live with us rent free; Ivan who spends all his time here from three in the afternoon till late at night . . . and father. All of them extremely nice and cheerful people but vain and full of themselves, always talking, stamping their feet, and with never a penny in their pocket.

(He could lose his temper too.) They hung on to the precocious son and brother like leeches—and by mixing his pride with his comic sense, he hectored and coughed them into order. Although he was broad and strong as a young man, he was soon in bad health; he is the classic case of the doctor and consumptive who refuses to admit his case and neglects it.

On top of all this, Chekhov found time to write over 4,000 vivid letters, many of them merry, many of great literary importance, to critics, editors, novelists, friends and to women who were in love with him and whom he was evading. The notion of the melancholy, passive, defeated Chekhov vanishes when one considers these letters alone, and especially when one meets the candour, spontaneity, the humour sharp as horseradish and the intimacy of his correspondence. The man is alive to the tips of his fingernails and has the knack all good letter writers have of springing in person before the reader's eyes. In letters a writer projects a large number of impromptu disguises, and, since he was often secretive in a self-preserving way, we do not get the whole of Chekhov—whatever that was—but we always see him in the hour he is living through.

A few of Chekhov's letters were published soon after his death. They were followed by a six-volume edition edited by his sister who adored him though she did make decorous cuts. There followed some of his letters to his wife, the actress Olga Knipper whom he married in the last years of his life. In 1948–1951 an official Soviet collection appeared and was revised and expanded in 1963–1964 to the number of 4,200 items. From this edition Avrahm Yarmolinsky has extracted some 500 of the 'most telling'—helped by the excellent translator Babette Deutsch. In another edition Michael Henry Heim and Simon Karlinsky have selected 185. Heim is the translator and Karlinsky gives a thorough critical commentary.

The editors of the two new volumes speak gratefully of the work of the Soviet scholars but cannot conceal their amusement or irritation with the well-known vagaries of Soviet censorship. The Russians have long been prudish about sex and the bodily functions, and in these matters Chekhov was often outspoken and sportive: after Pushkin (Simon Karlinsky points out), Russia became genteel as did the West, but the censorship in the Soviet Union has, uniquely, held on to nineteenth-century prudery. In a passage like:

> There is no outdoor privy here. You have to answer the call in nature's very presence, in ravines and under bushes. My entire backside is covered with mosquito bites,

the word 'backside' has been deleted.

In matters of ideology, Chekhov's admiration of certain things in the West to the detriment of Russian efforts has been cut—yet not always in every edition. But here, when one considers how subversive Chekhov's ideas on artistic and personal freedom are, and how generally opposed to the tenets of official doctrine in the Soviet Union, the tolerance of the editors surprises. They pay their tribute to Caesar by cutting out what Chekhov said about the superiority of European actors to Russian actors, and other matters that offend Russian chauvinism, but the rest suffers little. The American editors have not found it difficult to put back much of what may have been tampered with.

The two selections of the letters now offered overlap, particularly in the important ones. Both volumes are well annotated. After a short and pleasant introduction the Yarmolinsky edition leaves Chekhov to speak for himself. There are more of his letters to his wife, Olga Knipper, than in the Heim and Karlinsky edition: they bring out more variously the harassed passion of the one powerful—and belated—love of Chekhov's life; and the letters written during the Sakhalin journey convince one of the revival of Chekhov's vigour. Both editors dismiss the notion that the journey to Sakhalin was undertaken because of a love affair with Lydia Avilov: they agree with Ernest Simmons that the lady imagined the affair when she wrote her book. (Chekhov would be the last man wholly to gratify the lady or indeed our curiosity on the point.)

The smaller Heim and Karlinsky selection is critical and informative and is framed in a general thesis. They group the letters in periods, each section preceded by an account of Chekhov's growth as a writer from phase to phase, so that the background is set out in some detail. This is invaluable. They are particularly concerned with his hostility to the long socio-political tradition of Russian criticism and the misapprehension this has caused. Where Yarmolinsky calls Chekhov 'the incomparable witness', they go deeper into the nature of his witness. They show that the precocious success of Chekhov at the age of twenty-eight annoyed the intelligentsia because he was held to be a man 'without principles'—which infuriated him: his belief in the freedom of the artist was a principle. They also show why, in the later years of fame, his opponents adroitly denigrated him by defining him as the moody, twilit poet of futility and despair. They were too partisan to see his truthfulness and grace.

Since then many Soviet critics have seen him as an incipient revolutionary and have even distorted his language to demonstrate this. Through either blindness or disingenuousness, they mistake the nature of the one or two apparently directly political stories—*The Anonymous Man* or *The Bride* for example—which are not dogmatic assertions. In a well-known letter Chekhov said that it was not the artist's business to solve questions, but to pose them correctly. Marxists do not allow the posing of the question: they state the answer first and then create the question. Chekhov wrote when he was twenty-eight:

> I am neither liberal nor conservative, nor monk, nor indifferentist. I would like to be a free artist and nothing else and I regret God has not given me the strength to be one ... Pharisaism, dull-wittedness, and tyranny reign not only in merchants' houses and police stations. ... I see them in science and literature among the younger generation. I look upon tags and labels as prejudices. My holy of holies is the human body, health, intelligence, talent, inspiration, and the most absolute freedom imaginable, freedom from violence and lies, no matter what form the latter two take.

Or in a letter to Pleshcheyev about *The Name-Day Story*:

> It's not conservatism I'm balancing with liberalism—they are not at the heart of the matter as far as I am concerned—it's the lies of my heroes with their truths. ... You told me once my stories lack an element of protest and that they have neither sympathies or antipathies. But doesn't the story protest against lying from a start to finish? Isn't that ideology?

And in defence of *Mire*:

> A writer is a man bound by contract to his duty and his conscience.

These replies are a defence against the accusations of the orthodox radicals who accused Chekhov of selling himself to the reactionary millionaire Suvorin and his paper. He was at once critical of Suvorin and his grateful friend.

Here we come to the continuous argument of the Heim and Karlinsky book: Chekhov was a subversive writer in the Russia of the Eighties and Nineties. He was exceptional in not belonging to the gentry class: he was one of the few writers—Leskov was another—whose elders had come from below. Although he was opposed to Tsarism, his opposition had not been formed by the radical tradition of the literary intelligentsia, that is to say the tradition which, starting with the great Belinsky, demanded a didactic social content in literature and which was continued by Chernyshevsky, Pisarev and Dobrolyubov. (Lenin admired the last of these for turning a discussion into a 'battle cry, into a call for activism and revolutionary struggle'.) Chekhov believed that the radical utilitarians (with the exception of Belinsky) neither liked nor understood literature, and he was 'as subversive of the sociological presuppositions of a Russian Populist such as Mikhailovsky as of the Christian mysticism of Lev Shestov'. He was accordingly attacked for 'lack of social relevance', Karlinsky says, and the letters confirm him, that

> ... politically the most subversive aspect of Chekhov's thinking is his systematic demonstration of the illusory nature of all labels, categories and divisions of human beings into social groups and social classes, which are the starting point of all political theories of his time and ours.

The explanation is that Chekhov's intellect had been formed by the medical and biological sciences: his well-known practical work in hospitals, in building of schools, in the new local councils and in the clinics in the fight against cholera, brought him a great deal closer to the people and gave him a deeper knowledge of them than most writers of the time had. This has been awkward for some Soviet critics. In *The House with the Mezzanine*, the girl Lida (one of them complains) is doing exactly what Chekhov was doing in real life: dedicated social work. Yet Chekhov exposes her as an authoritarian and political fanatic who brutally wrecks her idle sister's life and he makes the reader admire the sweeter, weaker girl. In life Chekhov would no doubt have admired Lida's work. But, as Karlinsky says, he sees that Lida is a fanatic who will not tolerate opposition and indeed wishes to dominate the family. She will use any means to break those who oppose her beliefs. The story is not an attack on social concern but on the inhumanity and tendency of a particular humanitarian.

Chekhov's independent response to the pressure of the orthodox left-wing establishment is that of the working doctor: he is modestly self-accusing. He is bothered by abstract programmes and speculations. He wishes he were a 'great writer'. The best writers, he says,

> . . . are realistic and describe life as it is, but because each line is saturated with the consciousness of its goal, you feel life as it should be in addition to life as it is, and you are captivated by it. But what about us? We describe life as it is and stop dead right there. We wouldn't lift a hoof if you hit us with a whip . . . there is an emptiness in our souls. We have no politics, we don't believe in revolution. . . . No one who wants nothing, hopes for nothing, can be an artist.

That Chekhov was influenced for a time by Tolstoy's teachings —especially by the idea of non-resistance to evil—is true: but he soon returned to his own nature. As an artist he exposed himself. His purpose as a man was practical and he admired the intelligentsia when they went out to the villages and fought the cholera epidemic. One has the impression that the power to believe—in the doctrinal sense—was destroyed in his childhood by the violence and tyranny of his father: 'What aristocratic writers take from nature gratis, the less privileged pay for with their youth'—though they have had the triumph of their liberation. Unprotected by radical doctrine, Chekhov nevertheless exposed himself as an artist to the full misery of Russian poverty in such stories as *The Ravine* or *The Peasants* which may have been prompted by his reading of Zola. (He read widely in European literature.)

The Peasants is less a story than a collection of incidents that convey what poverty is like, in the sense that it is a sub-culture of its own. Everything depends on the choice of the right detail and showing it as an aspect of living. A broken Moscow waiter decides to move back with his parents and children to the home where he was brought up in the country. His childhood memories have deceived him. How to describe the crucial shock of arrival? Chekhov describes him looking into a filthy hut, not a house, but a shed half-filled with a dirty stove, covered with soot and flies on which a ragged girl is sitting. The parents are out in the fields and the child says nothing:

A white cat rubbed itself against the fire irons on the floor. Sasha [the waiter's child] beckoned to it.
'Puss, puss. Come here pussy.'
'She can't hear,' said the little girl. 'Deaf.'
'Why?'
'Someone hit her.'

By a single line we are prepared for squalor, rancour, drunken fighting, the rabid greed of poverty, the blaspheming grandmother, the loose-living daughter who comes home stripped of her clothes. A neighbouring hut catches fire and no one knows how to put it out; the tax collector comes for arrears and takes the samovars from every hut. He is an obsessive collector of samovars and lines them up in his own place. One young girl can read and, in a conceited way, breaks into Gospel reading. Yet there is nothing Zola-like in Chekhov's descriptions of the vile: they are not rhetorically vile. The waiter dies and his wife and her child leave to beg on the road. The wife thinks:

Yes, they were frightful people to live with. Still, they were men and women, they suffered and wept like men and women,

44

and there was nothing in their lives for which an excuse could not be found. . . . She now felt sick with pity for all these people and kept turning back to look at the huts.

What is striking about *The Peasants* is that Chekhov was able to catch every small drama in the lives of the community he describes in thirty pages.

One suspects that Chekhov's worry about 'purpose' had a good deal to do with his inability to write a long novel; he complained that he could not sustain a philosophic plan. The truth is that he lacked the novelist's vegetative temperament; he was avid for new beginnings and new 'good-byes'. His one serious attempt to write a long novel—it was scrapped after two or three years—collapsed from what he called 'fatigue' and because of the 'unreasoned' overcrowding of events, places, people, motives.

> Oh if you knew what a wonderful subject for a novel sits in my noodle. What wonderful women, what weddings, what funerals! If I had money I would make off to the Crimea, seat myself under a cypress and complete a novel in two months. . . . However, I am lying; if I had money in hand I would live it up.

Even in writing his stories he complained that he was a man of splendid beginnings who went flat from exhaustion in the middle and did not know how to go on. This self-criticism is of course absurd when one considers his very long stories *Ward 6*, *The Duel*, *Lady With a Dog* or *In the Ravine* in which he is certainly as great an artist as Tolstoy. Karlinsky quotes the hero of *Dr Zhivago*:

> Of things Russian, I love now most of all the childlike quality of Pushkin and Chekhov, their shy lack of concern over such momentous matters as the ultimate fate of mankind and their own salvation. They understand all that very well, but they

were far too modest and considered such things above their rank and position.

The letters indeed show that Chekhov did 'understand all that'. He attacked Suvorin, his friend and editor, on two crucial occasions: for the anti-Semitic articles Suvorin published at the time of the Dreyfus affair and the trial of Zola, and for Suvorin's attitude to the student riots of 1899:

No one can pass judgment in print on the disturbances when all mention of the facts is prohibited. The state forbade you to write, it forbids the truth to be told, that is arbitrary rule. . . . Right and justice are the same for the state as for any juridical person. If the state wrongly alienates a piece of my land I can bring an action against it and the court will re-establish my right to that land. Shouldn't the same rules apply when the state beats me with a riding crop?

About anti-Semitism at the time of Dreyfus:

Little by little a messy kettle of fish began stewing, it was fueled by anti-Semitism, a fuel that reeks of the slaughterhouse. When something is wrong we seek the cause from without and before long we find it: it was the French who messed things up, it was the Yids, it was Wilhelm. . . . Capitalism, the bogeyman, the Masons, the syndicate and the Jesuits are all phantoms, but how they ease our anxieties. . . .

Even if Dreyfus were guilty,

Zola is right, because the writer's job is not to accuse or perse-cute but to stand up even for the guilty once they have been condemned and are undergoing punishment. 'What about politics and the interests of the state?' people may ask. But major artists and writers should engage in politics only enough to protect themselves from politics.

As Karlinsky says, Chekhov's greatness does not lie in what he said about the culture of the time, indeed he often contradicts himself. It lies in his invention of 'dazzling literary forms' and particularly in finding a way of seizing the dramatic value in our very inability or unwillingness to communicate fully with each other. Rather pretentiously Karlinsky elaborates this as 'the semantic tragedy', and 'the changes in the texture of time's fabric which cause every attained goal to be different from what it was at the planning stage and which make a teleological approach to any undertaking or any personal relationship an absurdity'. What Chekhov saw in our failure to communicate was something positive and precious: the private silence in which we live, and which enables us to endure our own solitude. We live, as his characters do, beyond any tale we happen to enact. So, in the saddest as in the most sardonic of Chekhov's tales, we are conscious of the simple persistence of a person's power to live out his life; in this there is nothing futile. What one is most aware of is the glint of courage.

The letters do not say much about the making of this fabric. The most we learn is that his head was packed with people, that his early trash, as he rightly called it, was written by a very bright reporter and for money. Chekhov began by laughing at his stories. In 1883, in his 'trash' phase, he told his elder brother how to write a short story:

1) The shorter the better.
2) A bit of ideology and being up to date is most à propos.
3) Caricature is fine, but ignorance of court and service ranks and of the seasons is strictly prohibited.

In 1886, when the serious Chekhov first appeared, the instructions were drastic and in fact describe almost any good story he ever wrote:

1) Absence of lengthy verbiage of political-social-economic nature.

2) total objectivity.
3) truthful descriptions of persons and objects.
4) extreme brevity.
5) audacity and originality: avoid the stereotype.
6) compassion.

He hated publicity and the pushing of his career. He was a self-perfecter and resented that he had to make money. He was an enormously responsible man who liked to pass as a reckless fellow. He was very susceptible to women and, indeed, said wine and women always set his imagination going. He wrote with more sympathy and understanding of women and was more their liberator than any other Russian writer except Turgenev. His many love stories are really woman stories in which the women are presented whole. If his own love affairs were generally short, his affection for the women concerned was lasting. Love did not turn into hatred. He was by nature too restless, too hard-working to be either a resounding romantic amorist or a compulsive seducer. He would marry, he often said, if he could be sure that the lady and he could arrange to live apart. Such love letters as survive are a mixture of fantasy, playfulness and farcical insults—'There is a great crocodile ensconced within you, Lika'—and are really letters of friendship, in which his determination on his own independence is frank but unwounding.

One understands his curious, defensive insistence that the 'sad' plays are not only comedies but in fact farces. He is asserting that life is a fish that cannot be netted by mood or doctrine, but continually glides away between sun and shadow. And this feeling, his letters show, is at the bottom of the value he put on his freedom. Gorki reports that Chekhov did not like conversations about 'the deep questions with which our dear Russians assiduously comfort themselves'. And he certainly did not like the 'Chekhovians':

Once a plump, healthy, handsome well-dressed lady came to him and began to speak à la Chekhov. 'Life is so boring, Anton Pavlovitch. Everything is so grey: the people, the sea, even the flowers seem to be grey. . . . And I have no desires . . . my soul is in pain . . . it is like a disease.'

'It is a disease,' said Anton Pavlovitch with conviction. 'In Latin it is called *morbus fraudulentus.*'

Like a great many, perhaps all Russian writers of the nineteenth century, Chekhov caught people at the point of idleness and inertia in their undramatic moment when time is seen passing through them and the inner life exposes itself unguardedly in speech. He caught people in their solitude.

The comedy of Chekhov lies in the collisions of these solitudes. That is why, despite Stanislavsky and the Moscow Arts Theatre, Chekhov insisted that his plays were not dramas, not tragedies, but comedies and even farces. The tragedy, if there was one, lay in the very fact of farce: and the farce existed because it displayed people speaking innocently out of their own natures; the gigantic Pichchik believes he is descended from Caligula's horse; he calls out, astonished at himself, in the middle of a dance that he has had two strokes; he cries like a baby when he says goodbye to his friends. He is acting out his inner life. It is at once farcical and sad that a man has an inner life.

We shall misunderstand Chekhov if we do not grant him this starting point. Again and again his impulsive letters help to bring this out.

TOLSTOY

The Despot

THE LIFE OF Tolstoy is a novel that might have been written
by Aksakov in its beginning, by Gogol in the middle and by
Dostoevsky in the years following the conversion. He was not
so much a man as a collection of double-men, each driven by
enormous energy and, instinctively, to extremes. A difficulty
for the biographer is that while we grin at the sardonic comedy
of Tolstoy's contradictions and are stunned by his blind egotism, we are also likely to be infected by his exaltation: how is
this exclamatory life to be brought to earth and to be distri-
buted into its hours and days? And besides this there is the
crucial Russian difficulty which the Russian novel revels in and
which mystifies ourselves: there seems to be no such person as a
Russian alone. Each one appears in a crowd of relations and
friends, an extravagantly miscellaneous and declaiming tribal
court. At Yasnaya Polyana the house was like an inn or cara-
vanserai. There is the question of avoiding Tolstoy as a case or a
collection of arguments. And the final affront to biography is
the fact that Tolstoy exhaustively presented his life nakedly in
his works.

One's first impression of Henri Troyat's remarkable Life is
that we have read all this before and again and again, either in
the novels or the family's inveterate diaries. So we have, but
never with M. Troyat's management of all the intimacies in the
wide range of Tolstoy's life. He was a man always physically on
the move, even if it was only from room to room; even if it
was simply gymnastic exercise, riding, hunting at Yasnaya
Polyana. He is in Petersburg or Moscow, in the Caucasus, in

Georgia, in Germany, England, France and Italy; and when he moves, his eyes are ceaselessly watching, his impulses are instantly acted on. His military career, his wild life, are packed with action and mind-searching. In sheer animality he outpaces everyone; in spirit and contradictions too. The amount of energetic complexity he could put into the normal search for a girl to marry, outdoes anything that the most affectable sentimental novelist could conceive. Marriage, when it did come, was abnormal in its very domesticity. M. Troyat writes:

> Sonya was not sharing the destiny of one man but of ten or twenty, all sworn enemies of each other; aristocrat jealous of his prerogatives and people's friend in peasant garb; ardent Slavophil and Westernising pacifist; denouncer of private property and lord aggrandising his domains; hunter and protector of animals; hearty trencherman and vegetarian; peasant-style Orthodox believer and enraged demolisher of the church; artist and contemptuous scorner of art; sensualist and ascetic . . .

M. Troyat has managed to make this live with the glitter of the days on it. His book is a triumph of saturation. He has wisely absorbed many of Tolstoy's small descriptions of scene and incident and many of his phrases into the text. So when Tolstoy rushes off to one of his outrageous bullyings of his aunts in Moscow, we are at once back in a drawing room scene in *Resurrection*; and one can see M. Troyat going adroitly to the novels for exact moments of the life. He has learned the master's use of casual detail. He has learned his sense of mood and also of 'shading' the characters. He does not lose an instance of the ironic and even the ridiculous in Tolstoy's behaviour, but—and this is of the utmost importance—he keeps in mind the tortured necessity of Tolstoy's pursuit of suffering, and his knowledge of his situation. The conscience of the prophet often performs farcical moral antics, but fundamentally its compulsions are tragic. One can be angered by Tolstoy's hypocrisies, but also know that they agonized Tolstoy himself.

A test for the biographer is the exposition of Tolstoy's great quarrels. They are so absurdly jealous that the temptation must be to leave them in their absurdity. M. Troyat does better than this. The row with Turgenev, the breach and the reconciliation years later when Turgenev had become a garrulous old man, has never been so well-placed and made to live, as in this book. The comedy of the reconciliation brings laughter and tears to the eyes. There Tolstoy sits at the family table making enormous Christian efforts to repress his undying jealousy of the elegant and clever man who enraptures the family. Tolstoy grunts while Turgenev shows the girls how one dances the Can Can in Paris. It is a farce that contains the sadness of the parting of irreconcilables; even more than that, for Turgenev is a dying man and does not fear death. He is interested in his disease and is sure that death is the end of all. The still vigorous Tolstoy is terrified of death; his flesh demands immortality. The search for God, was really a return to childhood, an attempt at rejuvenation, but in Turgenev, Tolstoy was faced by a man who lived by an opposite principle. At thirty-five Turgenev had hit upon the infuriating device of attaining serenity by declaring his life was over, and then living on as a scandal until his sixties. One is present at a country house scene in a heart-rending play by Chekhov, where the elders are tortured and the young people laugh.

The story of Tolstoy's marriage is one of the most painful stories in the world; it is made excruciating by the insane diary-keeping of the parties. They exchanged hatreds, crossed them out, added more; from the very beginning the habit of confession was disastrous and brutal. Like the Lawrences and the Carlyles, the Tolstoys were the professionals of marriage; they knew they were not in it for their good or happiness, that the relationship was an appointed ordeal, an obsession undertaken by dedicated heavyweights. Now one, now the other, is in the ascendant. There is almost only one genial moment, one in which the Countess conquered with a disarming shrewdness that put her husband at a loss. It occurs when the compromise about the copyrights is reached. The Countess decides she will publish her share of his works herself and consults Dostoevsky's widow, who has been very business-like in a similar undertaking. The two ladies meet enjoyably and profitably; the Countess is soon making a lot of money, she is happy—to Tolstoy's annoyance. The art he had denounced was, as if by a trick, avenging itself on his conscience. He was made to look foolish and hypocritical. And yet, after all, they were short of money and his wife had proved she was right.

If there had been no struggle for power between the couple—and on both sides the feeling for power was violent—if there had been no struggle between the woman who put her children and property first and the man who put his visions before either; if there had been no jealousy or cruelty, there was enough in the sexual abnormality of both parties to wreck their happiness. Even though mere happiness was their interest for only a short period of their lives. She hated sexual intercourse and was consoled by the thought that by yielding to his 'maulings', she gained power; and he, whose notions of sexual love approached those of primitive rape, hated the act he could not resist. His sexuality tortured him. He hated any woman after he had slept with her. Conscious of being short and ugly, he was appalled that women were magnetized by him. Into this question—so alluring to psychologists—M. Troyat does not go very far; he simply puts down what is known and, of course, a great deal is known. It is an advantage, and in conformity with his method, that M. Troyat has not gone on the usual psychological search. He would far sooner follow Tolstoy in his daily life, tortured by lust or remorse, than dig into the unconscious. The fact is that Tolstoy seems to have known something nearer to love in his devotion to his aunts and to one or two elusive and distinguished older women.

About the Works M. Troyat has many interesting things to say. Because he was many men Tolstoy was able to get into the skins of many men, and the Countess understood that he was most fulfilled and made whole by the diversion of his protean energies into imaginative writing. On that she is unassailable; even his messianic passion produced religious fables of great purity and beauty; and in *Resurrection*, the recognition of the moral integrity of the prostitute is a triumph of Tolstoy's psychological perspicuity in a novel that does not promise it. Tolstoy's fear of death had a superb imaginative expression in *The Death of Ivan Ilich*—but, it is to be noted, this was not written in one of the passionate phases of his life, but in a period of coldness that was almost cynical. M. Troyat has a sentence which describes Tolstoy's love of quarrelling and his promise to reform, but only for the pleasure of going back on his promise, a sort of moral slyness, which contains a comment on his nature as an artist:

> Impenitent old Narcissus, eternally preoccupied with himself, he blew on his image in the water, for the sheer pleasure of seeing it come back when the ripples died away.

It is at the rippling stage, when he has dissolved himself, that he is an artist. And, of course, very conscious of what he is doing. He is watchful as an animal that sees every surface movement, he builds his people from innumerable small details of things seen. A misplaced button may tell all. He 'shades'—that is to say, he builds out of contradictory things: a cold dry character will be shown in a state of surprising emotion partly because this is true to nature, but also because that gives him an extra dimension that will surprise the reader. Tolstoy rewrites a scene again and again in order that the reader shall not know in the course of a conversation whose side he is on. He makes a great point of impartiality. Although *Anna Karenina* strikes the reader as a novel with a clear idea, set out in orderly manner and of miraculous transparency, the fact is that Tolstoy did not know what he was going to do when he started, and many times, in altered versions, changed the characters and the plot. He groped very much as Dostoevsky did, though not in a fog of suggestion, but rather among an immense collection of facts. The Countess and her daughters had to copy out many versions and the printers found on his pages a mass of re-writing which even Balzac cannot have equalled. One can see—and this is true of many artists—that the trivial idea from real life takes its final form only as the subject is finally assimilated to the self or experience of the author. He is edging towards a vicarious self-analysis.

It is fitting that this Life should have been done in Tolstoyan fashion with constant attention to the vivid and betraying surface. Not a single incident among the thousands of incidents fails in this respect. Yet the whole is not novelized. There is no imagined dialogue: it finds its place out of the immense documentation. The commentary is ironical, but a just sense of the passions involved is there: perhaps M. Troyat leans more to the side of the Countess but she is drawn as a woman, not as a cause, and we see her change, just as we see Tolstoy as an incalculable man. The complexity of the long final quarrel and the flight is made clear, and the narrative, at this dreadful point, is without hysteria. One can't forget such things as the old man sitting on a tree stump in the wood, secretly altering his will; or the Countess rushing out half-naked to pretend to drown herself in the pond. Then comes that awful train journey in the Third Class: the dim, inadequate figure of the worshipping doctor who went with Tolstoy; the whispers of the passengers who knew they had the great man with them; the bizarre scene at the station when the Press arrived and were not allowed to take pictures of the station because it was illegal to photograph railway stations: the face of the demented Countess at the window as she looks at her dying husband to whom she is not allowed to speak—the whole scene is like the death of a modern Lear. As Isaiah Berlin wrote in *The Hedgehog and the Fox*, Tolstoy

> died in agony, oppressed by the burden of his intellectual infallibility and his sense of perpetual moral error: the greatest of those who can neither reconcile, nor leave unreconciled, the conflict of what there is with what there ought to be.

GONCHAROV

The Dream of a Censor

ON THE FACE of it, it is extraordinary that one of the great comic novels of the Russian nineteenth century should have come from the hand of the most pedestrian, industrious and conservative of state officials, Ivan Goncharov, a man outwardly devoid of fantasy and lacking inventive powers. From what leak in a mind so small and sealed did the unconscious drip out and produce the character of Oblomov, the sainted figure of nonproductive sloth and inertia; one of those creatures who become larger and larger as we read?

The simple view—still held by some Soviet critics and encouraged by remarks of Goncharov himself—is that *Oblomov* was a solemn exposure of the laziness and ineffectiveness of the landowning class; but as it grew in the slow process of the writing (which took between ten and thirteen years) the novel became far more than that. Several contemporary critics have even suggested a prophetic kinship with Beckett and have noted the protest against the work ethic that has created a sense of emptiness and boredom in the modern world. Everyone exclaims at the influence of *Don Quixote*, to which Russian novelists so often responded; but, thinking of Goncharov's case, one could say that it is just as extraordinary that the Cervantes of the neat *Exemplary Novels* should also have burst the formal bonds of his period. All one can say is that literature has a double source: one in life, the other in literature itself, and if one is going in for the influence game, Goncharov's admiration for *Tristram Shandy*—the corresponding English comedy of domestic lethargy—may have helped to awaken his dilatory and very literary mind. From Sterne he learned to follow a half-forgotten tune in his head.

The interest of a new study of Goncharov by Milton Ehre lies in his close knowledge of Russian critical writing and his observation of the detail of Goncharov's impulses and methods as a novelist. *Oblomov* appears to be a work of objective realism as minute in this respect as a Flemish picture done from the outside, yet in fact it comes from the inner secret anxiety of an organized, even carefully dulled temperament. This anxiety arises from a haunting nostalgia for what has been lost, an edginess suggesting fear of a hidden 'abyss' that lies close to one who, torn between the ideal and the practical, has opted for the respectable golden mean.

There is, at times, an air of fret in Oblomov's nature that makes him seem on the brink of madness from which surrender to his sloth, perhaps, saved him. This madness came out in the form of paranoia in Goncharov himself toward the end of his life when he accused Turgenev and even Flaubert of stealing his ideas. Goncharov was State Censor and, maybe, the man who had such political power over the works of his contemporaries had been quietly boiling with the jealousies of the unconscious and the temptations of a right-thinking profession which hates the imagination. Censors go mad, just as prison governors come to feel, as prisoners do, that the only righteous people are those inside. The curious fact is that the unconscious of Goncharov, a lifelong bachelor, pushed him in old age into a fate like Oblomov's: will-less, drowsy, isolated, petulant, fond of food, he surrendered himself to the care of his manservant's widow, whom he called his 'nursemaid' and 'little mother', and he left his fortune to her and her children, whom he had virtually adopted.

Before making his closely analysed study of Goncharov the artist who wrote only three novels in his life, Professor Ehre points to the important wounds and compensations in the personal story. It is a little like Gogol's, if it is less harrowing. It has some not dissimilar seeds of instability, and since Goncharov's writing was very autobiographical—and in this sense unimaginative—the real life is important. He came from a well-off family of the merchant class—and was the child of the second marriage of an elderly man and a girl of nineteen. The father died when the boy was seven, and a rich relation of the landowning class, an educated man of the world, took charge of the family. This Tregubov is one of the sources of the character of Oblomov. The boy had thus two fathers: the real one, a religious fanatic, dedicated to ritual and Byzantine formalism, and a melancholic; the other, an aristocrat, an intellectual, a humanist, a disciple of Voltaire and the Enlightenment, full of charm and totally indifferent, in the manner of the Russian landowners, to the practical demands of running his large estate at Simbirsk, a region often ridiculed for its sleepy and comic provinciality.

The place was an Oblomovka in itself and is precisely evoked in Oblomov's famous dream: one of the almost beautiful fantasies in Russian literature. As so often happens in countries where the males are denied a ruling political role, the women become the power figures: Goncharov adored his mother who was, however, one of those strict and practical Varvara Petrovnas who rule the Russian novel. She saw severely to his education, got him to Moscow University, and fitted him to become the efficient civil servant he eventually became. He was nevertheless uneasy in aristocratic company—rather jealous too—and among talented contemporaries like Belinsky, Herzen and Turgenev he was obliged to be only a spare-time writer. The truth is that his upbringing and temperament were as much to blame as his feeling of social inferiority for the neurotic indecisiveness which plagued and protracted his attempts to write. Indecisiveness also ensured that his one known love affair—the model for Oblomov's love of Olga—should fizzle out. There is a failure to adapt romantic idealism to natural feeling and action, to give up the pleasures of talk for the risk of the deed; the personality is split and, in the end, the deep boredom or ennui so familiar in Russian literature of the time becomes a sort of governing secret society in his nature.

Such maladies can be an enormous advantage to the man who can goad himself into the writing of a masterpiece. Cold, cold, cold, Chekhov complained of Goncharov; but knowing he had talent, susceptible if not inventive, turning self-mockery into play, frightened of the possibility of losing his talent, Goncharov dragged on year after year, forcing *Oblomov* to become a work of art. It is typical of the paralysing indecisiveness of his nature that he was working on another long novel, *The Precipice*, at about the same time and that while *Oblomov* was a study of stagnation almost without direct narrative and plot, *The Precipice* was sternly political and acted out with crude bad temper in dramatic episodes. This book was a failure.

But it would be wrong, as Professor Ehre shows, to think of Goncharov groping or blundering in his methods. The most revealing chapters of Ehre's study are those that follow in detail Goncharov's clear understanding of what he was doing, and the principles he stuck to and the value he put upon the need to allow memory and the unconscious to ripen and form his work. He knew he was a conservative artist, that a form in which life stood still was indispensable; that he was dealing in types which would cease to be types and become symbols, that the more realistic his scenes were the more subjective must be the moving force.

In the chapter on the novelist's aesthetic views, Ehre quotes two passages from Goncharov's letters that show he had an exact notion of what he was doing and that *Oblomov* is not an oddity blown up to sprawling proportions:

[The writer] should write not from the event but from its

reflection in his creative imagination, that is, he should create a verisimilitude which would justify the event in his artistic composition. Reality is of little concern for him.

Art represents nature as a refracted image. Reality was too 'varied' and 'original' to be taken as a whole. He said much the same thing in a letter to Dostoevsky. If the Western calendared attitude to plot and precise action escaped him, he had on his side the Russian sense of the hours of the day running through his scenes and people like a stream or continuous present.

Since I do not know Russian I cannot comment on Goncharov's style and its rhythms, though I do see that plain or average styles such as his have to be consciously achieved. Writers who have no style are as obtuse as people who have no manners, either good or bad. Since Oblomov, like all extreme or outsize characters, is on the point of being mythical, I can, with some resistance, almost accept Ehre's references to Freud in his comments on Goncharov's relationship with his mother as suggesting the sun, warmth, a refuge from the Petersburg winters; and I can also see that if one looks back on childhood as an Arcadia one will have to recognize that one of the attractions of childhood is that it is lived under a system of magical rules whose chief use is that they give shelter to the imagination.

But we do not enact myths only in our lives. It is just as satisfying when thinking of Goncharov's difficulties in love to attribute these to the influences of Romanticism, in which it was natural even in split personalities both to idealise and fear 'ladies' as distinct from 'women'. Goncharov solved his difficulty by the ironic mockery of his feelings, i.e., by playing the game of being a man of the world. Oblomov, after all, is reluctant, not sexless but sly. In his early comedy of manners, *A Common Story*, Goncharov was content with the ironic reversals of idealism in love and to show, with some relish, the price of worldliness: the young hero becomes as cynical as his uncle—a Tregubov figure—and the uncle attempts disastrously to re-cover the follies of his youth and heart. But in *Oblomov*, the novelist broke out of this neat formula, with the result that the critics have been divided by the account of Oblomov's love of Olga and her marriage to Stolz; and Ehre is very suggestive.

At first reading Stolz is a virtuous stick and Olga is not much better; at later readings, Olga strikes one as being a remarkable portrait of an unformed sentimental girl acquiring the will of a real woman, and one can take the whole episode as a very penetrating study of the deceits of Romanticism in its watery mid-century form. When Oblomov falls into the arms of his servant and has children by her, Stolz feels the sluggard is lost and has taken the plunge into the 'abyss'. He has, so to say, gone native and Stolz breaks with him; but Olga begins to see him as one who, resisting the modern world's worship of will and activity, has preserved the quality called 'heart'. Perhaps Oblo-mov is self-indulgent; but Stolz remains stolid, and one under-stands, in theory, Olga's unrest in her sensible marriage to a responsible man.

If we accept this, it remains true that the Olga-Stolz episodes are unsatisfactory, but for another reason: one of style. How important that tune in the head is! The moment we get away from Oblomov himself the narrative becomes flat and toneless: as Ehre says, it becomes dry, argued, and conceptualized. One can even suspect here he had stolen from Turgenev a theme that was beyond his own sensibility.

Goncharov's unconscious had no living or literal material to offer when marriage or romantic love were the subjects. In his next novel, *The Precipice*, all the petulance and jealousy came out in the ageing Censor. He could not use the tongue of the younger generation. His particular genius lay in the prolonged and loving farming of his only aristocratic estate: his private evil.

DOSTOEVSKY

The Early Dostoevsky

WHEN DOSTOEVSKY WAS a cadet in the Academy of Engineers—the story runs—he designed a nearly perfect fortress, but forgot the windows and doors. A guide to the novels: the reader is dropped into the novelist's claustrophobia, and it must be said that the enormous amount of Dostoevsky criticism since 1880 makes the walls thicker. The task of tunnelling one's way out of his labyrinth is exhausting, and there is disappointment (if there is also relief) in discovering that the great artist was often, like Balzac and Dickens, also a journalist who skids into a phantasmagoria of 'the topical and *au courant*'.

This is a phrase of the Czech critic Václav Černý: all the critics have their phrases. We are helped for a moment and then we are forced to discard: the *âme slave* was the first to go; it was followed by Dostoevsky as 'the key' to the Russian character; we hesitate over the surely conventional theory of Dostoevsky as the product of medieval Russia in collision with capitalism. Too many 'ideas' occur to us. The root of the trouble is that the artist, the man in the act of writing, is lost—he was before anything else an improvising artist. As Mikhail Bakhtin put it in his well-known and difficult book, *Problems of Dostoevsky's Poetics*, which first appeared in Russian in 1929 and was expanded in 1963,

> The subject is not a *single* author-artist, but a whole series of philosophical statements made by *several* author-thinkers— Raskolnikov, Myshkin, Stavrogin, Ivan Karamazov, the Grand Inquisitor and others. . . . The critics indulge in polemics with

63

the heroes; they become their pupils, and they seek to develop their views into a completed system.

Such criticism is concerned with ideology alone and not with the evolving storyteller, at home in the slipshod but struggling against it, and autobiographical to the point of apotheosis.

For the biographer who sticks for the moment to the early pre-Siberian Dostoevsky, as Joseph Frank does in *The Seeds of Revolt*, the ground is clearer. (There are three volumes still to come.) The great novels are not yet here to obscure the man whom Siberia enlarged and transformed. We are able to see the young man painfully growing. The story has gradually become well known, but it still contains its mysteries and Mr Frank's very long book can be called a work of detection and collation at its scrupulous best. Every detail is considered; evidence is weighed and fortunately the author has a pleasant and lucid style, unleadened by the fashionable vice of fact-fetishism. He brings a clearer focus and perspective to things that have been often crudely dramatized, especially in Dostoevsky's childhood and youth, and we have a more balanced and subtler account of this period than we generally get.

There is no prophetic assumption, for example, that Dostoevsky's father was a rough, miserly, flogging, lecherous brute like the older Karamazov. The home itself could not be the source of Dostoevsky's knowledge of abandoned or lethargic poverty. Childhood was happy, if youth was not. The anxious father was ambitious, energetic, strict, but thought constantly of his children's piety, education, and future; the mother was deeply loving. The boy had his father's energy and determination and dash. Where was the flaw that made both father and son unstable, jealous, envious and instantly suspicious? When one looks at Dr Dostoevsky's past one sees how powerfully he was influenced by the dream of rank and advancement; even his narrow religion was the dreaming sort of dissident Puritanism which urges the family up the social ladder. This was very much a nineteenth-century dream. The worm in the heart of Dr Dostoevsky's success in achieving rank in the lowest grade of the Russian nobility was the knowledge that he had been merely admitted to the new service 'aristocracy' invented by Peter the Great and could never become part of the traditional gentry, in fact or in his attitudes.

The crowded Dostoevskys lived very much to themselves. They dwelled in the legend—perhaps it was a fact—that their forebears in the sixteenth century belonged to the old Lithuanian gentry class. Their history has a suggestive religious aspect. The ancient Dostoevskys were scattered and divided in nationality and creed.

The Orthodox Dostoevskys, falling on hard times, sank into the lowly class of the non-monastic clergy. Dostoevsky's paternal great-grandfather was a Uniat archpriest in the Ukrainian town of Bratslava; his grandfather was a priest of the same persuasion; and this is where his father was born. The Uniat denomination was a compromise worked out by the Jesuits as a means of proselytizing among the predominantly Orthodox peasantry of the region: Uniats continued to celebrate the Orthodox rites, but accepted the supreme authority of the Pope. Dostoevsky's horrified fascination with the Jesuits, whom he believed capable of any villainy to win power over men's souls, may perhaps first have been stimulated by some remark about the creed of his forebears.

The debate about reason and faith would have had an ancient edge and force to it if it ever occurred in the doctor's small apartment in his hospital. The Dostoevskys differed from the real gentry in a more important respect. The real gentry had become merely lax in religion and tended to be sceptical Voltaireans. Aristocrats like Tolstoy and Turgenev had had no religious education. But for Dostoevsky:

The very first impressions that awakened the consciousness of the child were those embodying the Christian faith. . . . Dostoevsky was to say that the problem of the existence of God had tormented him all his life . . . it was always emotionally impossible for him ever to accept a world which had no relation to a God of any kind. . . .

If aristocrats like Turgenev's mother flogged their sons, the domineering doctor never once struck his children. Whether he flogged his serfs when his new status allowed him to own land and he bought a poor estate in the country is not really known; but he sent his elder sons to a private school in order to shelter them from brutality: until then he had been their strict schoolmaster. He saw they were taught Latin and the indispensable French well.

Yet if the childhood was happy, it lay under a lid: the strain of the father's anxiety for rank and success became hysterical after his wife's death. He had awakened a deep love of literature in his children, yet, still pursuing conventional status, sent Feodor to the Academy of Engineers against the boy's will. The Academy was a great drain on his pocket and the father was so beside himself that he had a stroke when Feodor failed to be promoted in his first year. Feodor became extravagant and wanted, in his turn, to cut a 'noble' figure, and we get the first signs of duplicity and guilt in the sanctimonious begging letters to the father.

At this point Mr Frank deals with Sigmund Freud's famous essay on the Oedipal nature of Dostoevsky's conflict with his father. Freud believed Feodor had become parricidal and, in fantasy, homosexual; and that his epilepsy now occurred as a discharge of the guilt he felt when his father, now deep in drink, was murdered by his serfs. (Dostoevsky's silence on this subject is extraordinary, and indeed the murder did not, in any case, become known until long after his death. It had, for respectability's sake, been hushed up.) Freud's case was easily demolished by E. H. Carr in his *Life* published in 1931. Mr Frank agrees with Carr and believes that Dostoevsky's disease did not appear until just before his imprisonment in Siberia or just after. If he was mentally ill in adolescence this is likely to have been so because, like his father, he had little control of his nerves and his temper.

In the ambivalence of Dostoevsky's relations with the father he resembled, and in his fluctuations between resentment and filial piety, Dostoevsky had his first glimpse of the psychological paradox. He came to seek 'self-transcendence, a sacrifice of the ego', and, says Mr Frank, 'whether one calls such a sacrifice moral masochism, like Freud, or more traditionally, moral self-conquest', is a matter of terms.

We move on to the early struggles of the writer and a far closer view of the literary scene than the foreign reader is usually given in other Lives. Russian culture in the 1830s was moving from German Romanticism and Idealism towards French Realism or Naturalism. The influence of George Sand, Balzac and Victor Hugo on young Dostoevsky was enormous (he translated *Eugénie Grandet*) and in Russian literature so were the influences of Pushkin and Gogol. We move on to the conflict with Belinsky who had praised *Poor Folk* and to the interminable debates on socialism with or without free will and Christian faith that lead us eventually to the Petrashevsky conspiracy, the climax of the trial at which Dostoevsky declared, 'Socialism is a science in ferment, a chaos, alchemy rather than chemistry, astrology rather than astronomy.' Mr Frank goes on to quote from the *Memoirs* of Alexander Milyukov, who suggests that there was a small Populist wing in the Petrashevsky group and that this is where Dostoevsky may possibly be placed.

The account of the Petrashevsky meeting is given at length, and if Mr Frank is not vivid—others *have* been—his account is gripping as a piece of detection among ideas. For 'What are your convictions? What are your ideas?' set the note of discussion in the many 'circles'—satirized at the time by Turgenev—that were characteristic of a society where there was no freedom of the press. Dostoevsky wandered in and out of these discussions, occasionally bursting out with emotional attacks on the tsarist bureaucracy, but in the main he simply floated giddily among the Radical speakers. Only one political question preoccupied him passionately: the emancipation of the serfs. The tsar himself was hesitating in the matter.

There was a change in Dostoevsky when the extraordinary, dramatic figure of Speshnev appeared among the drab and circuitous intellectuals. A few years earlier in his life Dostoevsky had been bowled over by the perfect aristocrat: Turgenev ('I love him'). Speshnev, too, was an aristocrat; wealthy, cultivated, travelled, cold and strong. His melancholy feminine appearance fascinated (Semenov remarked that 'he could well have served as a model for the Saviour'). He was to become the model for Stavrogin in *The Devils*.

There is the report of Dostoevsky's doctor, who found the novelist irritable, touchy, ready to quarrel over trifles and complaining of giddiness. There was nothing organically wrong, the doctor said, and the trouble would pass. 'No, it will not,' Dostoevsky said, 'and it will torture me for a long time. I've taken money from Speshnev'—500 rubles in fact—'and now I am *with him* and *his*. I'll never be able to pay back such a sum, and he wouldn't take the money back; that's the kind of man he is. Now I have a Mephistopheles of my own.'

Speshnev was a sinister example of 'the double' who brings about catastrophe. The money, of course, was meaningless to Dostoevsky, the perpetual borrower, living the hard life of an unsuccessful writer; it was the will of Speshnev that was irresistible. It drew him towards what he abhorred—some form of revolutionary activity. What appalled him, Mr Frank argues, was that he had, in his unstable way, lost his moral freedom. Later in life he told his second wife that but for the *providential* accident of his arrest he would have gone mad! The strange thing is that living for contradictory extremes, Dostoevsky was one of those neurotics who recover their health and even their serenity when disaster at last occurs.

Mr Frank's first volume stops with the arrest and trial. The last hundred pages deal with the novels and stories Dostoevsky had written up to this point. If we except *The Double* and *White Nights*, these belong to the Dostoevsky few people read, for although there are flashes of talent, they are derivative of Gogol, Hoffmann, Sand, clumsy in construction, garrulous and tedious. Mr Frank is conscientious in his hunt for signs of a developing moral insight, but I am afraid his exhaustive summaries of the stories and the examinations of the characters do not make the tedious less so. In one Hoffmannesque tale of incest and demonic possession, *The Landlady*, one does see (as Frank says) a new theme emerging: the crushing of the personality under traditional Russian despotism and, in the portrait of Katerina, there is his first study of masochism. (Katerina says, 'My shame and disgrace are dear to me . . . it is dear to my greedy heart to remember my sorrow as though it were joy and happiness: that is my grief, that there is no strength in it and no anger for my wrongs.')

When one tackles these stories, one has to admit there is a certain mastery and even a tenderness in evoking masochistic sensuality. But one also sees how this derives from literature. He had not read the Gothic novels in vain; he was a great borrower and already an expert in pastiche and parody. *Netotchka Nezvanova* is Russified George Sand and is for me, though not for Mr Frank, unreadable. It has the turgid air of obsessive conspiracy which certainly became a characteristic element of Dostoevsky's genius, but here the artist is cramming too much in. The one thing I miss in Mr Frank's reading is a real response to Dostoevsky's comic irony, although he does praise the brilliant hack's pastiches of the bedroom farces of Paul de Kock.

Dostoevsky was surely, from the beginning, a master of dialogue and situation, and one of the great comic wits. His morbid insight into psychological contradiction, his habit of seeing the conflict of inner and outer life, not only as a quest but an imbroglio, are constantly attended by the sardonic spirit when he reached the height of his powers. And it is in this, rather than in his religious or moral utterances, whether they are subtle or overweening, that one feels the iron quality of for-giveness which elsewhere is sentimental.

'Without art,' Dostoevsky once wrote, 'man might find his life on earth unlivable.' And, one must add, he might find the novelists and, above all, a certain kind of academic critic, hard labour. In Mikhail Bakhtin's *Problems of Dostoevsky's Poetics* the originality of this great Soviet scholar's work is obscured by a structuralist prose so opaque that one has to translate to oneself as one struggles on. An inventor of awful words in Russian— 'characteriology' for example—he has been a great trouble to his apologetic translators. But Bakhtin does understand that Dostoevsky is creating his own means as an artist. For him Dostoevsky is the inventor of a new genre, the polyphonic novel. His characters are not the author's voiceless slaves but rather 'free people who are capable of standing *beside* their creator, or disagreeing with him, and even of rebelling against him'. There is a plurality of voices inner and outer, and they retain 'their unmergedness'.

He goes on:

> Therefore the hero's word is here by no means limited to its usual functions of characterization and plot development. . . .
> The hero's consciousness is given as a separate, a *foreign* con-sciousness. . . .

The traditional European novel is 'monological', a thing of the past, and if Dostoevsky's novels seem a chaos compared, say, with *Madame Bovary*, so much the worse for the tradition. Man is not an object but another subject. As for Dostoevsky's ideas, they are

> artistic images of ideas: they become indissolubly combined with the images of people (Sonya, Myshkin, Zosima); they are freed from their monological isolation and finalization, becoming completely dialogized and enter into the great dialogue of the novel on completely equal terms with other idea-images (the ideas of Raskolnikov, Ivan Karamazov and others). . . .

Dostoevsky's principle as a novelist is simultaneity. There is no doubt that Bakhtin exactly describes the originality of Dostoevsky; one has indeed the impression of being among people whose inner lives are dangling at the ends of their tongues. The lasting defect is that so much self-dramatization drives one into the ground. Not all tongues are equal. Polyphony suffers from the excess of voices. Only in *The Brothers Karamazov*, where the effect is of theatre, has Dostoevsky really brought them to order. Where Bakhtin becomes most stimulating is in his remarks on Dostoevsky's shameless indulgence in literary genre: the detective novel, the story of adventure, parody, pastiche, boulevard farce, grotesque and melodrama. Dostoevsky has prolonged periods of seeing life as an enormous scandal or as a revival of the ancient folk traditions of Carnival in which the types are contemporary and not mythical.

At this point Bakhtin takes a long, effusive, learned flight into the history of the scandalous Carnival tradition and is immensely suggestive. It is delightful to see a scholar going too far. I am surprised to read that these scenes in which—to use Bakhtin's metaphor—the drawing room becomes a public square, are thought by many critics to be artistically unjustified. Surely, no longer? They are at the height of his comic achievement. This kind of scene is organic, nothing invented in it (as Bakhtin says), though when he says such scenes really go back to the 'underworld naturalism' of the menippea of Petronius and Apuleius, I enjoy the scholarly trapeze act but I don't believe a word of it.

On the whole, European criticism of Dostoevsky has not paid much attention to him as a novelist at work; it has concentrated on his ideas. This is natural: the hunger for apocalypse has recurred, reviving, exhausting itself and reviving again, in every decade of this century as the human situation gets worse. One can see why Dostoevsky, the prophet and 'gambler who doesn't dare not to believe' is still the master; he moves forward with us as the sense of our own danger changes. We reject, as people fifty years ago did not, his preaching of the Russian Christ which so blandly overflowed into military chauvinism, for the notion of the man-God was Victorian and Dostoevsky's irrationalism offered us something unpleasantly close to the herd-God of fascism. But we were left with his insights into Russian history. When the West recovered from the catastrophe that he had accurately prophesied, there was still the great psychologist of the 'mystery of man'. And when that required counter-checking, we now find in him the authority on such strange elements in the Russian character as the communal personality and the morbid habit of confession. If anyone took up alienation as a profession it was he.

Yet we would not be reading him at all if he had not wrenched his great and his minor novels out of the chaos and contradictions of his own mind by a strictly artistic process. He was a novelist first and last. His very characters are storytellers. It is the novelist who contains the prophet, the sensationalist, the rather smug hair-raising journalist and the often disingenuous mystic. To an exalted and agonized lady who thought he, above all, surely must know the synthesis that would heal the dualism tormenting her, he replied cheerfully that dualism has its delights as well, and that, for his part, he was lucky: he could always turn to writing. A wise remark, but one does have the impression that the gambler who played for the highest spiritual stakes had an unfair resource when he had lost all his money.

One turns therefore to a Russian critic for a sharper, native view of these matters. Professor Mochulsky died in Paris in 1948 and his admired book on Dostoevsky appeared in Paris the year before. A professor at Odessa and the Sorbonne, Mochulsky experienced a religious conversion and became a disciple of Berdyayev. For the reader who expects a new approach to Dostoevsky, this is ominous news. We have already had so much about Dostoevsky's spiritual struggles. Ernest J. Simmons, E. H. Carr and others had already used most of the immensely important notebooks, letters and journals which were available, and have made economical and skilful use of them; they caught also some of Dostoevsky's irony. And although Mochulsky does, in minute detail, shows us the novelist struggling to arrive at his 'idea', changing and re-changing his plots and his characters until the idea becomes plausible life, we are far more aware, in the end, of the message than we are of the novel. It is no news that Dostoevsky's novels are dramas of conscience and belief; but they are great novels because he is able to translate this into specific acts and scenes of believing, and because he creates imbroglios of extraordinary physical vividness. He is a sculptor of molten figures.

Of course, it is important to see how the famous conflicts arose (the love-hate in the conflict with Belinsky, the utilitarians and the humanists; with the landowner tradition and the effect of being forced into the company of criminals) and he forged the contradictions of belief and nature into people; but there is far too much synopsis in Mochulsky's book, and far too little exposition of Dostoevsky's power of theatrical scene, of his gift of hallucination, his narrative whose strongest effects somehow arise from their disorder; and there is not enough about his humour and comedy. A hurried but classically constructed novel like *The Eternal Husband* might be a conscious parody of the great tragedies; but it points to the barbed, sardonic laughter which makes his pages of exaltation, or tortured doubt and terror, finally human. The recurrence of the great scandal scenes—on which Mr Ronald Hingley was very good in *The Undiscovered Dostoevsky*—and indeed the fact that nearly all Dostoevsky's characters are seen in a scandalous light for his own purposes and even by compulsion, are matters which a less religious critic would have attended to. And there are questions like Dostoevsky's ability to put a whole houseful, a whole set of people, an officeful, on the page instantly. This is his *biographical* gift. Life stories of endless complexity hang shamelessly out of the mouths of his characters, like dogs' tongues, as they run by; the awful gregariousness of his people appears simultaneously with the claustrophobia and the manias of their solitude. Dostoevsky contrives always to select so that he is able to show everything happening at once, without freezing into dead statement, and without thereby exhausting his subjects at the outset. Dostoevsky's sense of time is a sense of bursting, continuous instants. A whole life, past and present, breaks open this minute and will go on bursting in every minute that follows.

Some of these things *are* implicit in Mochulsky's analyses of the books and he is properly aware that since Dostoevsky is a confessional writer, the links with his own dramatic life are important. He was experienced in finding enemies to whom he could glue himself, upon whom he could fawn, and with whom he could fight. Like the saints, he knew how to hit below the belt. Mochulsky knows that the novelist is theatrical—one can often grasp Dostoevsky far more easily on the stage than in the novels—that he is poetic, that his struggle to find a form for his work was part of the spiritual struggle; that he is, as he said, an expressive rather than a descriptive artist—one of the reasons for his attraction today. Mochulsky is good about his literariness, about Dostoevsky's growth out of literary forbears like

Gogol, Hoffman, Balzac, Hugo; the importance of Shakespeare, Cervantes and of Dickens. He was much swayed by foreign writers. He welcomed confusion. One sees him switching from an intended novel called *The Drunks* to *Crime and Punishment*, stopping to write *The Gambler* in a month and then putting *The Drunks* into *Crime and Punishment*. Raskolnikov was at first to be another Rastignac. The novel was to be a first person confession; this was abandoned for an outside narrator. Initially in *Crime and Punishment* the idea was to be that crime leads to moral rebirth and redemption. Suddenly Rastignac is replaced by Napoleon and we have Dostoevsky's involvement with the 'strong' character and the questions of pride, power and living beyond good and evil. At the end of the novel he looked for a compromise that would reconcile his conflicting ideas about Raskolnikov's fate:

> The 'vision of Christ' and his heroism at the fire had to be discarded; Svidrigailov and not Raskolnikov fell heir to the solution of suicide. An exterior dénouement still remained; his giving himself up to the authorities, the trial, his deportation to the penal colony; but this did not suffice for an interior spiritual development. Raskolnikov did not repent and did not 'rise' again to a new life. There is only a promise of his resurrection in the concluding words of the epilogue . . . 'the miracle-working force of life will sustain him' . . . The murderer has not yet been saved, but he can be saved if he will completely give himself up to a spontaneous, irrational love of life.

The changes in the conception of the character of Prince Myshkin are even more extraordinary. At first he is quite the opposite of the final character: he is to be a power figure, a spiritual brother of Raskolnikov. (Dostoevsky swings giddily from one extreme to the other.) Myshkin is to be an epileptic. Then he is to be like Iago—another instance of a bookish choice —cold, envious, vindictive; after a glance at Turgenev, the enemy, he becomes 'a superfluous man', an idle power. Then he turns into a Stavrogin, a character whom we see trying to be born in other novels. After that he is the opposite, the 'holy fool'. Dostoevsky is really looking for the most dangerous solution. He finds it in 'a beautiful individual'—Christ, Don Quixote, Valjean—even Pickwick is considered. The idea was never certain for him until the fourth part of the novel and he was harassed by the feeling that the Prince ought to be, like Don Quixote, a comic character.

And, in fact, it is as a comic character that he almost succeeds. Dostoevsky's nearest approach to Quixote (though a more mundane one and untroubled by selflessness and the imagination; he is simply bullied and is an old liberal with out of date ideas) is the figure of Stepan Trofimovitch Verhovensky in *The Devils*. He is a reminder that there are periods of untheatrical tolerance and ripeness in Dostoevsky. There was a good deal of the sinful humanist left in the mystic; a good deal of slyness, of never quite letting the right hand know what the left was doing. It is here that prophet and novelist come together.

Mochulsky is clear that Dostoevsky is without landscape, is uninterested in nature, ignorant of peasant life—which makes nonsense of his mystical exaltation of the Russian people. Much to the taste of the Symbolists and some contemporary critics is the suggestion that he was seeking to enact basic human myths: 'the enchanted bride', 'the revolt against Mother Earth', 'the stranger'. He certainly portrayed the Man-God and the Covetous Knight. I find Mochulsky most informative about Dostoevsky's style: it is a talking style in which his own voice and the voices of all his characters are heard creating themselves, as if all were narrators without knowing it.

PUSHKIN

Founding Father

IT IS SAID that among foreigners only the Baltic Germans can see Pushkin's genius as a lyrical poet at once. The rest of us who have no Russian and read his poetry in English or French translation echo the remark made by Flaubert to Turgenev—'Il est plat, votre poète'; it expresses our polite embarrassment before a mystery. To the dramatic poet-novelist in *Eugene Onegin*, to the prose tales and above all to his marvellous letters, we do respond. In the last we hear the natural voice of the man that goes leaping along beside the cooler voice of the conscious artist and we at once see why the Russians think him the greatest of their letter writers. He is there before us: 'In casual letters of confession/One thing inspired his breath, his heart/And self-oblivion, was his art!/How soft his glance, or at discretion/How bold or bashful there, and here/How brilliant with his instant tear'. We learn to 'mourn for Russia's gloomy savour, Land where I learned to love and weep'. We see the courtier trapped by the Court; we see the rake who wears his nails long and who looks like a monkey, the aristocrat of two aristocracies: the Court and Art; the patriot who, like the Spanish Cid, is struggling with a false king. Pushkin had the art of appearing suddenly dishevelled or elegant, out of the very hour he was living. He is as concise as impulse itself. He is as clear as ice, as blinding as snow.

It is true that a lot of Pushkin's letters are mystifying—who are all these people? What is it all about? By now biographers have picked out the important ones, but it is still startling in the three volume edition translated into English by an American

77

scholar, J. Thomas Shaw, to find how all still have their instant upon them and bring out Pushkin's voice. It is a good idea to have a life of Pushkin handy when reading them; but Professor Shaw's exhaustive notes pin down a long list of minor writers, actresses, mistresses, social figures and officials, and point the detail of adventures, projects and scandals. A half-elegant, half-barbarous scene is there if one can piece the fragments together; and when this is too much for us, Pushkin is there from youth to just before his death, never failing in accent or gesture. His mood, because it is so changeable, switching at every sentence, may seem careless at first. Looked at more closely almost all the letters are as certainly works of art as the letters of Byron are.

Pushkin has the appetite for life and, more important from a letter-writer's point of view, a genius for playing with it, for changing his tone, for leaving some things sardonically unsaid and others spoken bluntly. He is entranced by his laughing mastery of all kinds of style from the drily formal, the eloquent, the witty to the hotly argued and tenderly felt. He enjoyed rewriting. He was a keen tester of phrase. Each sentence rings like a true coin. For the moment he is all ours and we, on hearing him, are all his.

Here he is held up in quarantine because of the cholera and distracted because of the family quarrels concerning his marriage:

All you say about society is just: all the more just are my fears that aunts and grandmothers and little sisters may start turning my young wife's head with folderol. She loves me, but look, Aleko Pletnov, how *the free moon goes its way*. Baratynsky says that only a fool is happy when he is a fiancé, but a thinking person is disturbed and agitated about the future. Up to now it has been I . . . but now it will be we. A joke! This is the reason I have been trying to hurry my mother-in-law along; but she, like a peasant woman of whom only the hair is long, did not understand me and was fussing around about a dowry; to hell with it! Now do you understand me? You do? Well, thank God! . . . I should like to send you my sermon for the local peasants on the cholera; you would die laughing, but you do not deserve this gift.

Pushkin is not one who, self-entranced, takes one underground into the labyrinth of introspection. He takes it for granted that he is known and that we know what it is to be a man. He is modest. He is expressive but neither tortuous nor exhibitionist. His stress is not on the egotist's 'I' because he is multifarious. He writes rather as the messenger or familiar of a human being called Pushkin who, though perpetually in some sort of scandal or trouble, is like a swimmer who knows how to survive in a storm of his own making and who will make no fuss if he sinks. The appetite for life is not simply a matter of extroversion; it is inseparable from the appetite for putting it into words. Yet he does not live in words alone. Once every three days he is in love with a new woman; he is quarrelling with the censorship, travelling on awful roads, drinking, gambling, listening to his old nurse, eagerly describing his poems, amusing himself in villages, flung into bouts of inspiration, driven forward by whim, never frosted with doubt and never green with guilt or remorse. These, he says, he never felt. He looks like a monkey and is as lithe and restless; and he has a touch of dangerousness too. He insists that he is an aristocrat. But he insists, too, that he writes to make money, for that frees one from the servilities of patronage.

Pushkin's biographers have all pointed to the powerful self-control he must have had and the letters show that he has reserves; but one thinks of him not so much as a man wrestling with his passions or in conflict with himself, but one who is in command of his experience. He is inhabited by a genius that guarantees his integrity; but his is not a mad genius: it is sane, orderly, generous, serene in feeling. It is impossible to imagine ourselves trusting the judgment or good sense of a Dostoevsky or a Tolstoy. Egotism distorts them. Pushkin one entirely trusts. He is so open. His follies expose the corruption of the society he lived in, rather than falsity in himself. Pushkin lived very much like other men of his class, very much in the world. The early letters are those of a brilliant, dissipated character living the loose life society willingly allowed to the young and well born.

> Everything is going as before; the champagne, thank God, is lasting—the actresses likewise—the former gets drunk up and the latter get f . . . Amen. Amen.

To women 'who have too much sense to be prudes', he writes with flattery and innuendo:

> I shall imitate a monkey, I shall slander, and I shall draw for you Mme de . . . in the 36 poses of Aretino.

(Professor Shaw, who belongs to the exhaustive tradition of American editing, does not forbear from telling us that Aretino's erotic work has 38.) To Mme Kern, one of his mistresses who wants to leave her husband, Pushkin writes

> My God, I'm not going to preach morals. But yet respect is due to a husband, else nobody would want to be one. Do not oppress the vocation too much, it is necessary in the world.

There is a more dangerous female who was to be with Pushkin all his life:

> Give my greetings to the censorship, my ancient girl. I do not understand what in my elegiac fragments could have troubled her chastity . . . One may and must deceive the old woman for she is very stupid.

In obtaining the right to be censored only by the Tsar, who

used the pretext of saving Pushkin from himself, the poet saw he was caught in a cruel comedy that was to be played out coldly to the end of his life.

> They deprive me of the right to complain (not in poetry but in prose, a devil of a difference) and then they forbid me to be enraged . . . The right to complain exists in the nature of things.

At thirty young men of Pushkin's class were expected to marry and settle down. Obedient to convention Pushkin settled down. The rake turned with sudden tenderness to the 'necessary vocation' of being a husband and enjoyed the novel pleasures of family anxiety. He was captivated. But he was caught between a rancorous mother-in-law, a cunning Tsar and a coquettish wife. His marriage which mellowed him also destroyed him. That was tragic and yet, of course, both as a man and an artist, Pushkin got what was vivid and valuable in his life and work from venturing; not from change itself, but from the capacity to make it. His vitality jumps out in every sentence. For one who scattered his life in storms and comedies, he is astonishing for a fundamental seriousness. And what he read! Byron, Shakespeare, Corneille, Goethe, Scott and Voltaire, of course. Racine to quarrel with and Mme de Staël to defend. He hated German metaphysics. But he knew enough about Addison and Steele and the system of patronage in English literature. He could recall lines from the low characters of Fielding. He treats literature as a form of action.

Even when he picks an obscure friend's poem to pieces, he enhances as he criticizes. His literary letters are entirely mixed in with the life of the moment:

> The next day I ran across Nikolay Raevsky in a bookshop. '*Sacré chien*,' he said to me with tenderness, '*pourquoi n'êtes-vous pas venu me voir?*' '*Animal*,' I answered him with feeling, '*qu'avez-vous fait de mon manuscript petit-Russien?*' After this we

set off together as if nothing had happened, with him holding me by the collar in plain sight of everybody, to keep me from jumping out of the calash.

This is from one of his letters to his wife, a touching correspondence beginning in awestruck devotion, going on to the tender, the possessive and playful and ending in the painful attempts to allay his dismay at her sexual coldness and her jealousy. It is a comedy in the French fashion, with a cold undertone and a dire end.

On one question that was to become crucial to later generations, the split between Westerners and Slavophils, he has a letter of great importance. The letter is a criticism of Chaadaev's famous pamphlet which argued that, having fallen into the hands of Greek orthodoxy, Russia had had no real history, culture or tradition. Chaadaev was arrested and declared mad. Pushkin wrote to him, before this official persecution occurred, agreeing with Chaadaev's attack on Russian social life, but rejecting the religious argument:

We have taken the gospels and traditions from the Greeks, but not the spirit of puerility and controversy. The customs of Byzantium were never those of Kiev.

This is the characteristic view of the man of the world: the Russian clergy are backward because they wear beards and are not in good society; then patriotism is stirred:

What? Are the awakening of Russia, the development of its power, its march towards unity (Russian unity of course), the two Ivans, the drama that began at Uglich and concluded at the Ipatiev Monastery—is all this to be not history, but a pallid and half-forgotten dream? . . . Do you believe that (the future historian) will place us outside Europe?

Pushkin was deep in European literature. He was avid for the remodelling of literary forms; in a *Selection* of his literary letters, another editor, Tatiana Wolff, says:

> When Pushkin wrote of his calling as a poet he did not write of afflatus: on the contrary he always wrote of himself as a crafts-man. The Muse was his gossip and his mistress with whom he did not have to be on the best behaviour—powdered and in pumps. The letters came in spate, full of comments on the books he had read, requests for more books, praise, blame, vituperation, enthusiasm. He questioned, argued and swore . . . There was a note of increasing urgency in Pushkin's determina-tion to replace the influence French literature had on Russian with that of German and English.

His letters are always dashing in their candour:

> I sing as a baker bakes, as a tailor sews, as Kozlov writes, as a doctor kills—for money, for money, for money—such I am in my naked cynicism.

When we turn to Pushkin's prose tales, the common opinion is that he writes in frozen, formal, well-corseted style that seals the subjects from the outside air. In a very fine study, *Pushkin: A Comparative Commentary*, Mr John Bayley disposes of this view, gracefully and with learning. Pushkin was indeed so deep in English and French eighteenth-century writing that it is per-haps natural to see that classical style as having been transposed without change when, in fact, he was a pillager of styles. He was, as Mr Bayley says, fascinated by the way in which modern literature had imposed its stereotypes on the men and women of the period, a process particularly marked in Russia where the upper class tended to identify itself with a current European model. 'It made a contrast, sometimes a grotesque one with the solid ramifications of Russian life.' Pushkin is less a giant than Proteus, as Shakespeare was, presenting new forms with the laughing boldness of a Renaissance figure. Form is of the greatest importance and it is on this subject, particularly—to my taste—in his discussion of *Eugene Onegin* and the prose tales, that Mr Bayley is most penetrating. For there is a paradox here: the strictly formal artist is one who brings to Russian writing the sensation we have that the doors and windows of the closed house are open and that more than one person lives there to tell its tale. The watching writer can make no rigid claims because he himself is watched by other selves within himself or, maybe, only by the sky:

> *Eugene Onegin* and *The Bronze Horseman* . . . have a formal per-
> fection and inevitability, combined in being provisional and
> open-ended, a paradox that has a parallel in the structure of the
> greatest Russian novels.

The carefully insured impersonality or evasiveness of the writing is warm: there is none of Flaubert's chill.

On the surface *The Queen of Spades* or *The Stationmaster* are no more than skilful anecdotes in an antique setting—which was one reason for Mérimée's regard for them. They emerge from 'old papers', hearsay or after-dinner talk, in the conventional manner, and a tale like *The Stationmaster* looks at first sight like a simple reversal of the Prodigal Son story, as it might be retold by Maupassant. On a second reading one sees that this is not so. At the end we do not give a shrewd grin at the expense of the poor stationmaster's mistaken belief that his daughter's 'fall' will be a moral disaster, when it has turned out to be a most respectable success. Indeed, the success is not the sort of paradox enjoyed by a man of the world, but is humanly moving. We see a life unexpectedly surviving the clever or stupid misunderstanding of experience, and compassion cuts the claws of irony. In the last lines of the flat ending, life, doubting life, assimilates not only father and daughter, but the narrator himself. The 'closed' end is really open. The same may be said of the far richer *Queen of Spades*, where the terse picture of a society and an obsession with meaningless luck can be read on several levels and where the curious Russian gift of exact portraiture-by-accident or devastating miniature puts an indelible glitter on the people. The story melts into the interests of other lives.

Pushkin was a constant literary collector, but he changed what he collected. He is an example of the writer who shocks old subjects into life by a gay and intelligent search for new means. It is interesting that the incident in *The Captain's Daughter* where the girl goes on a journey to the Empress to plead for the life of her betrothed was taken from the *Heart of Midlothian*, yet with what new dramatic ease or innocence of eye! The economy and the impudent bravura of these tales are shapely, but the sense of the open, passing hour is always there and it will pervade all the great Russian novels that follow.

The longest and most illuminating essay in Mr Bayley's commentary on Pushkin is the one on *Eugene Onegin*. To English ears the manner and the voice are Byron's and in the opening book Pushkin seems to be explicit. The young dandy is a fop, spending three hours before the looking glass, a pedant of fashion:

> Porcelain and bronzes on the table.
> With amber pipes from Tsaregrad;
> Such crystalled scents as best are able
> to drive the swooning senses mad,
> with combs, and steel utensils serving
> as files, and scissors straight and curving,
> brushes on thirty different scales;
> brushes for teeth, brushes for nails.

The loot of Paris and London. Then the sudden twist of irreverent comment

> Rousseau (forgive a short distraction)
> could not conceive how solemn Grimm
> dared clean his nails in front of *him*,

the brilliant crackpot: this reaction
shows freedom's advocate, that strong
champion of rights, as in the wrong.

He's off to Talon's, to hear the corks go flying up, as he sits
before his bloody beef, his truffles

and pâté, Strasbourg's deathless glory,
sits with Limburg, vivacious cheese
and *ananas*, the gold of trees.

He'll shout at the ballet, alarm the ballrooms. Don Juan is on
the prowl. Soon he will be Childe Harold, 'glum, unpleasant,
caught by the British *spleen* and the Russian *chondria*'. Who is
he? Is he Pushkin himself, or is he being Byron out of sheer
vivacity?

I regularly take much pleasure
in showing how to tell apart
myself and Eugene, lest a reader
of mocking turn, or else a breeder
of calculated slander should
spying my features, as he could,
put back the libel on the table
that, like proud Byron, I can draw
self-portraits only—furthermore
the charge that poets are unable
to sing of others must imply
the poet's only theme is 'I'.

This is Mr Bayley's moment. The autobiographical surgery of
Constant's *Adolphe* is in the poem; but Pushkin is deep in
Clarissa, in Fielding, Scott and above all in *Tristram Shandy*: he
is parodying the novel of sentiment. For Mr Bayley this poetic
novel is far more closely related to *Tristram Shandy* in form than
to *Don Juan*. As in *Dead Souls*, *Don Juan*, *Finnegans Wake* or *The
Waves*—Mr Bayley says—

The impression is one of constant and brilliant improvisation, problems and contingencies recurring in endless permutations . . . under the guise of a dazzling helplessness. . . . The author escapes at every moment into the new pattern of the structure that he is creating.

The poem is, so to say, one of the earliest anti-novels, and it is achieved by conscious art. Mr Bayley's great attraction is that he shows the pleasure of the poet at work and brings him closer to us by his asides. Pushkin shares with Joyce and Sterne

an easy relationship with poetic facility and cliché. What Wordsworth and the romantic poets forget in their stricture on the poetic diction of their predecessors, was that the best poets who used it never took it very seriously, just as a great rhetorician does not take the rhetoric he makes use of very seriously.

The clichés of Pushkin are 'aware of their own obviousness and emphasize it with gusto'. Another good comment, which takes one back to the 'openness' conveyed in this stylized work, is that *Eugene Onegin* is not depressing—certainly not in the manner of the nineteenth-century realists. The daily life of Russia in Petersburg and the country sparkle; and if ennui follows the frustration of love, recollection has its tenderness; there is a kindness in the acceptance of experience.

The very incomprehension of one character by another, the abyss of distance between them, is as much an earnest of possible happiness as of deprivation. When Tatyana says 'yet happiness was so possible, so near . . .' her words have something more than the pathos of illusion . . . The perspective of 'life's humble journey' opens out from every point in *Eugene Onegin* where artifice, irony and the patterning of the novel of sentiment are most dazzling and triumphantly in control.

Possibly the changes of mind Pushkin went through during the years of writing the poem were a help. More important are the nonchalant changes of point of view in the narration. The elusive narrator-within-a-narrator gives the poem that circular, round-and-round view which was to become common in the Russian novel, so that the personages are at once 'we' and 'I'. The sentiments, the passions, are a dream; we are mocked but without ill-will. We dream, we wake up. Time passes through us as we pass from youth to age. We are defined and re-defined as the days melt and remake us.

STRINDBERG

A Bolting Horse

AN INTELLIGENT EDITION of Strindberg's anti-feminist stories, *Getting Married*, has been done by Mary Sandbach. The commentary is detailed and valuable to those of us who have seen many of Strindberg's plays but who do not know him thoroughly as a prose writer and know even less about the tensions in Swedish life in the last half of the nineteenth century.

Among the Ancient Mariners who arrive to stop guests from getting into the wedding feasts of the European middle classes in that period, Strindberg has the most frenzied and unrelenting grip. The calms that lie between the bouts of paranoia are themselves dangerous. We can easily 'place' the sexual guilt in, say, *The Kreutzer Sonata*, for Tolstoy has immensely wider interests. But except, apparently, in his historical novels (which few people outside Sweden have read), Strindberg's personal obsession rarely ceases. He is the perpetual autobiographer who has at least three albatrosses—his three wives—hanging from his neck, and it is not long before he is telling us that the birds shot *him*. One of the surprising consolations of his life was that he liked going out into the country for a day's shooting, and it is a striking aspect of his lifelong paranoia in human relationships that he loved what he killed.

Strindberg's strange upbringing as the unwanted son of a successful businessman and a domestic servant, and as the victim of a stepmother; his poverty as a student; his quarrel with the Anabaptists and Pietists of a respectable society, who had him prosecuted for blasphemy because they hadn't the courage to bring him to court for his public campaign for sexual freedom;

89

his flight from literature into experiments with sulphur that drifted into a half-insane obsession with something like alchemy; above all, his instability as a husband or lover—all these torments kept him at white heat. What astonishes is the lasting fertility—in his work—of these ingeniously exploited obsessions. I can think of no other writer with the possible exception of D. H. Lawrence who retold himself in so many impassioned ways.

One thought one had seen his case analysed and dramatized for good in *The Father*—where he is the sea captain, in fact the Ancient Mariner in person, who was driven mad by the cunning calculations of a respectable bourgeois wife—or in *Miss Julie*. Yet, in 1903, much later, the whole personal story is retold as a legend, folk tale or saga for children, in the droll story called 'Jubal the Selfless'. This tale appears to be serene, but its playfulness and resignation are deceptive. The title itself is misleading. Jubal's selflessness is not that of the saints. It is the selflessness of an opera singer who, in old age, realizes that his ego or will has been systematically destroyed by a conspiracy between his father, his mother, and his wife (an actress who uses him in order to supersede him in his career). When he looks into his mirror—this is typical of Strindberg's brilliant theatrical imagination—he sees he is a body without a face. It is only when he finds his lost mother and puts his head in her lap that he recovers his ego—and, needless to say, dies!

The fable is a characteristic experiment with Strindberg's own history and it contains a truth about him as an artist and a person: the history and character are *disponible*. He is a model for the early nineteenth-century concept of Genius: the genius is free and without character but compelled to seek martyrdom. This is a matter for Strindberg's biographers. The work is far more important. Reading any story, particularly in the first section of *Getting Married*, one sees the link between the short story writer and the dramatist. He is a master in the use of overstatement; and one knows at once he is attacking a sententious and cliché-ridden society by the abrupt use of the offhand, natural voice:

> They had been married for ten years. Happily? As happily as circumstances allowed.

or:

> The couple met at dinner and at night, and it was a true marriage, a union of souls, and of two bodies into the bargain, but this they never mentioned, of course.

A young wife is fretting because she is not pregnant. The husband

> . . . had a confidential talk with his wife, and she went to see a doctor. Bang! Six weeks later the trick worked.

The word 'Bang'—used by many translators—seems to come, with a grin, from Strindberg the sportsman but it also shows his sense of theatre. A singer begins to get fat and to lose her audience—this is from 'The Tobacco Shed':

> She really began to get somewhat corpulent. She began so slowly and cautiously that she did not notice it herself until it was too late. Bang! You go downhill fast, and this descent took on a dizzying speed . . . the more she starved the fatter she got.
> 'It wasn't fat,' said the prompter. 'It was conceit.'

This devilish, grinning abruptness gives his stories a swinging elation. In play writing and story, the cutting from outside to inside the people has to be drastic and fast. There is no doubt of Strindberg's enormous talent; so that, in these stories, when he moves from one marriage to the next, one finds that as a realist with a message Strindberg is at ease in his mixture of the pugnacious, the pitying and the revealing.

Mary Sandbach says that Strindberg's misogyny has been overstressed; that he is as much concerned with the false values of a powerful upper merchant class which produces the unbending man and the cunning, idle female. His attack on 'Amazonian' women who wish to have careers or non-domestic interests is rooted in deep private jealousy of them—as in his first marriage—but he is talking of women who are 'idle' only because they have a huge supply of working-class girls as servants.

The message in the first series of the stories is that men *and* women must be liberated. In the second series, the excellent little scenes of life in town and country, the delight in the sea journeys and outings which bring out his high quality as an imaginative writer give way to arid, harsher analysis and polemic. But in the first part of one tale, 'The Payment', one gets that compelling and shrewd power of social analysis which D. H. Lawrence was to take further. The story is a full statement of Strindberg's case: the stifling of the sexual instincts leads women to use sex as a weapon, so that the men become the slaves while the women grasp occupational power outside the home. It must be read in the context of nineteenth-century life, but it approaches the Lawrence of 'St Mawr'.

Helène, the young woman in the story, is the daughter of a general. In her home she sees the exaggerated artifices of respect paid to women and grows up to regard all males as inferiors.

> When she rode she was always accompanied by a groom. When it pleased her to stop to admire the view, he stopped too. He was like her shadow. She had no idea what he looked like, or whether he was young or old. If anyone had asked his sex she would not have been able to answer, for it never occurred to her that a shadow could have any sex.

One day she is out riding in the country alone—she in fact hates nature; it makes her 'feel small'—and when she gets off her mare the animal bolts off to mate with a stallion before her eyes. She is shocked and disgusted. In the next phase she takes to the out-of-date library in her father's house and becomes infatuated with Mme de Staël's *Corinne*, and this leads her

> ... to live in an aristocratic dream world in which souls live without bodies. ... This brain-fever, which is called romanticism, is the gospel of the rich.

After the horse-riding episode, the analysis of the mind of a frigid, proud and ambitious girl as it grows degenerates into an essay, but it is nevertheless very thorough and alive. As Mary Sandbach says, 'For Payment' comes so close to the portrait of Hedda Gabler that many critics thought Ibsen must have read it. In the end Helène marries in order to trade on her scholarly husband's political reputation and get herself into public life: she is a recognizable high-bourgeois female type.

I think Mary Sandbach is right in disagreeing with those critics who say it is incredible that Helène's husband should submit to her rule even though, sexually, she has swindled him. This would be exactly in Strindberg's own character but—more important—there have been many observable and well-known instances of this armed frigidity since his day. Strindberg, the impossible, sincerely loved the recalcitrant woman, even if he reserved the right to take it out on her and then, with chronic masochism and double-mindedness, to crawl back for forgiveness. Strindberg's story fails not because it is false—emancipated groups, classes or individuals are often likely to be tyrannical and reactionary when they get power, as every revolution has shown—but simply because in the later part of this story the artist has been swallowed up by the crude polemical journalist. He has turned from life to the case book. Trust the tale, not the case history.

The original artist in Strindberg survives in his imaginative autobiographies, in the powerful and superbly objective and moving account of his breakdown in *Inferno*; in certain plays, and in the best of these stories. In many of these, a curious festive junketing, a love of good food and drink, a feeling for the small joys of Swedish life, and the spirit of northern carnival, break through. In 'Needs Must', the story of a bachelor schoolmaster who runs into a midsummer outing in the country and is eventually converted to a marriage which is very happy—'no part of this story', says Strindberg drily—Strindberg suddenly flings himself into the jollities of the trippers. The schoolmaster listens to the accordion and 'it was as if his soul were seated in a swing that had been set in motion by his eyes and ears'. It is a story that contains one of his happiest 'Bangs':

> Then they began to play Forfeits, and they redeemed all their forfeits with kisses, real kisses bang on the mouth, so that he could hear the smack of them. And when the jolly bookkeeper had to 'stand in the well' and was made to kiss the big oak tree, he did so with comical lunacy, putting his arm round the thick trunk and patting it as one does a girl when no one is looking, that they all laughed uncontrollably, for they all knew what you do, though no one would have wanted to be caught doing it.

If there is elation in the black Strindberg it springs like music out of his sunny spells. One is always compelled by something vibrant and vital in him. He is a bolting horse whatever direction he takes; and, as Mary Sandbach says, he brought new life to Swedish prose by his natural voice and his lively images. He was, as some have said, a cantankerous Pietist or Anabaptist turned inside out. His lasting contribution was his liberation of the language. The reader feels zest of that at once.

Estranged

AT THE BEGINNING of his Investigations of a Dog', Kafka wrote—in Willa and Edwin Muir's translation—

> When I think back and recall the time when I was still a member of the canine community, sharing in all its preoccupations, a dog among dogs, I find on closer examination that from the very beginning I sensed some discrepancy, some little maladjustment, causing a slight feeling of discomfort which not even the most decorous public functions could eliminate; more, that sometimes, no, not sometimes, but very often, the mere look of some fellow dog of my own circle that I was fond of, the mere look of him, as if I had just caught it for the first time, would fill me with helpless embarrassment and fear, even with despair.

The flat bureaucratic style strikes one as being a mask: Kafka notoriously did not know where he belonged. He was a Jew not quite in the Christian world; as a non-practising Jew—at the beginning anyway—he was not quite at home among Jews. The German critic Günther Anders, from whom I take these remarks, goes on:

> As a German-speaking Czech, [Kafka is] not quite among the Czechs; as a German-speaking Jew not quite among the Bohemian Germans. As a Bohemian he does not quite belong to Austria. As an official of a workers' insurance company, not quite to the middle class. Yet as the son of a middle-class family not quite to the working class.

In his family he wrote that he is 'more estranged than a stranger' and at the office he is alien because he is a writer. In love he is in conflict with literature. Because he was an extreme case which was exacerbated by fatally bad health, Kafka was able to enlarge, as by a microscope, the sense of exile which becomes visible as a characteristic of our experience in this century, its first martyr to 'alienation', which has become something of a cult.

When we turn from his books to his letters we have a series of self-portraits desperate and courageous, always eager and warm in feeling; the self is lit by fantasy and, of course, by drollery. His candour is of the kind that flies alongside him in the air. He was a marvellous letter writer. For these reasons alone the present translation of the *Briefe* first published in 1958 and collected by his great friend Max Brod is worth having. Richard and Clara Winston, the American translators, tell us that it is based on that volume and it is not clear to me whether 'based' means the whole or a selection from that volume—I fancy, the whole. (Other parts of Kafka's large correspondence have been translated, notably the important *Letters to Felice* by James Stern and Elisabeth Duckworth in 1973.) The present volume does contain now the full text of his long letter explaining his break with Julie Wohryzek to her sister, and the whole of the long letter to his parents a few days before he died in 1924 at the age of forty-one. There are also a few letters (of slight interest) to Martin Buber.

We hear the authentic Kafka when he is writing in a girl's album that words cannot carry memories because they are 'clumsy mountaineers and clumsy miners'; or to a fellow student when he is nineteen:

> When we talk together, the words are hard; we tread over them as if they were rough pavement. The most delicate things acquire awkward feet. . . . When we come to things that are not exactly cobblestones or the *Kunstwart* [a cultural magazine, of Nietzschean tendency, edited by a nephew of Richard Wagner:

another kind of paving], we suddenly see that we are in masquerade, acting with angular gestures (especially me, I admit), and then we suddenly become sad and bored. . . . You see, we're afraid of each other, or I am.

Later on, letters are comparable to 'mere splashings of the waves on different shores: the waves do not reach one'. In 1916, quick to admit that his stories are painful, he adds proudly that he wants to be 'truly a man of his time'. In 1922 when his many illnesses have united to become the fatal tuberculosis of the larynx, he writes to Robert Klopstock, the young medical student who was often with him in his last years, that he wants no indissoluble bonds, beyond the tacit, with men or women:

Is there anything so strange about this anxiety? A Jew, and a German besides, and sick besides, and in difficult personal circumstances besides—those are the chemical forces with which I propose to straightaway transmute gold into gravel or your letter into mine, and while doing so remain in the right.

That may sound bitter, but he is really thinking about his role as a writer of fables who reverses the classic manner of fable in order to be truly that man of his time. Again:

The writer . . . is a scapegoat of mankind. He makes it possible for men to enjoy sin without guilt, almost without guilt.

He sways between assertion and qualification, between reaching out to the gold of friendship and retiring into defensive strategies. They are necessary, especially in his relations with women, in order to pursue literature and nothing else. Such manoeuvres have a sick man's pedantry, but in fact the self-irony, the kindness, the nimbleness, the fantasy, mask the pain. When it is certain that he is terribly ill he begs that this shall be kept from his parents and adds that his earthly possessions have been on the one hand increased by the addition of tuberculosis, on the other hand somewhat diminished.

He imagines a battle of words going on between brain and lungs; talks of clinging to the disease like a child to the pleats of his mother's skirts. During a longish period at the house of his beloved sister Ottla at the village of Zürau he is plagued by country noises. A girl plays the piano across the street, children scream, men chop down trees, next comes the scream of the circular saw, then the loading of logs onto an ox wagon, the noise of the oxen, the shunting of the trains going away. A tinsmith starts hammering. Noise, he says, is the scaffolding within which he works; perhaps in the end, he says, noise is a fascinating narcotic. And then the house is alive with mice and the long half-farcical, half-obsessional drama continues for many letters. The creatures race round the room—he has the fancy that he can frighten them off by making his eyes glow like a cat's. He gets a cat in, the cat shits in his slippers; when the cat quietens the mice he still sits up half the night 'to take over a portion of the cat's assignment'.

Certainly this fear, like an insect phobia, is connected with the unexpected, uninvited, inescapable, more or less silent, persistent, secret aim of these creatures, with the sense that they have riddled the surrounding walls through and through with their tunnels and are lurking within, that the night is theirs. . . . Their smallness, especially, adds another dimension to the fear they inspire.

We see by his speculations about a Mouse Sanatorium that he is on the edge of one of his breakdowns and that soon he will once more find himself in hospital.

In love, Kafka sought perfection, knowing that it was an impossibility; knowing also the ideal served as a defence as ingenious as an insurance company's refusal to admit a claim. The most honest statement of this defence is in the long letter to Julie's sister, a confessional document of pitiless and subtle self-searching and, as always, frankly expressing his guilt—elsewhere he said that guilt so easily turned to nostalgia. The sincerity, and above all the sensibility to friendship, in letters to women, give them a spontaneous grace. The self he is preserving is in no way hard but clearly expatiated. Yet it glows under the friendship he receives and also offers.

As a sick man he is, one might say, negotiating a life which he knows is diminishing. He has the patient's ironical interest in the clinical state of his condition; and when he says, for example, that there is something fundamentally childlike in the Czechs of Prague, he describes a trait many foreigners have noted in the most tormented of all European cities, and a quality he shares. There is something of Italo Svevo, who was also partly Jewish, in his exploration of his condition: illness is a kind of second self that has cleverly moved in on him.

There is scarcely anything about the 1914–1918 war—illness secluded Kafka—although he does have a few incidental lines about the shortage of food and, afterward, some anxious joking about German inflation, especially in Berlin. He is even detached about anti-Semitism: this is interesting because it shows how active anti-Semitism was in the early Twenties in Germany; he makes a distinction between the Eastern European and the Western European Jews: the former were beginning to go to Palestine, to which he too was emotionally drawn and from which he withdrew: a spectator.

Kafka's most revealing things come most naturally in the letters to Max Brod, who is the strong, ever active, positive, generous and successful writer. Kafka reads Brod's latest works as they come out, comments on them with enthusiastic interest, and also takes over Brod's marital troubles in the manner of a brother exhaustive in advice. There is a letter to Brod in 1923, written from Berlin-Steglitz, which shows the continuous circling of Kafka's self-awareness:

It is true that I do not write to you, but not because I have anything to conceal (except to the extent that concealment has been my life's vocation), nor because I would not long for an intimate hour with you, the kind of hour we have not had, it sometimes seems to me, since we were together at the north Italian lakes. (There is a certain point in my saying this, because at the time we had truly innocent innocence—perhaps that's not worth regretting—and the evil powers, whether on good or bad assignments, were only lightly fingering the entrances through which they were going to penetrate some day, an event to which they were already looking forward with unbearable rejoicing.) So if I do not write, that is due chiefly to 'strategic' reasons such as have become dominant for me in recent years. I do not trust words and letters, my words and letters; I want to share my heart with people but not with phantoms that play with the words and read the letters with slavering tongue. Especially I do not trust letters, and it is a strange belief that all one has to do is seal the envelope in order to have the letter reach the addressee safely. In this respect, by the way, the censorship of mail during the war years, years of particular boldness and ironic frankness on the part of the phantoms, has proved instructive.

I forgot to add to my remark above: It sometimes seems to me that the nature of art in general, the existence of art, is explicable solely in terms of such 'strategic considerations', of making possible the exchange of truthful words from person to person.

Letters like this take one straight across the bridge from Kafka's private life into *The Castle* and *The Trial*, both of course unfinished and published after his death. There was a great deal of Swift (whom he read attentively) in Kafka's 'mad' imagination, above all in his habit of seeing people and sensations exactly, microscopically, as objects. He was much taken by

Swift's inflexible remarks on marriage and the bringing up of children. The letters to women have even something of Swift's advisory playfulness, and are all gentle to a degree one would have thought unlikely in a man so self-enclosed, alone, and perhaps even proud, with some delicacy of manner, of being incurable.

A Modern Nihilist

IN THE MOST literal sense of the phrase, Genet is a writer who has the courage of his convictions. Out of the lives of criminals, and following a tradition in French literature, he has built an erotic mystique, even a kind of metaphysic. Just as Zola was romantically stimulated by the idea of heredity as a fate, and by sex as a mindless habit of brutal instinct, so Genet is moved by an aspiration to the state of Absolute Evil. One thinks of him as a Vidocq without the gaiety, slipperiness and hypocrisy—a Vidocq who has read Dostoevsky; the autodidact of the jails.

Absolute Evil implies the existence of Absolute Good at the opposite extreme; but there is no sign of that in his writing. Absolute Evil is not the kingdom of hell. The inhabitants of hell are ourselves, i.e., those who pay our painful, embarrassing, humanistic dues to society and who are compromised by our intellectually dubious commital to virtue, which can be defined by the perpetual smear-word of French polemic: the bourgeois. (Bourgeois equals humanist.) This word has long been anathema in France where categories are part of the ruling notion of '*logique*'. The word cannot be readily matched in England or America, and simply has associations of the grotesque in Germany. Although 'bourgeois' has a definite place in Marxist hagiography, it is hard to appoint a certain place for it in our empiricism. Some believe that its emotional force in France comes from the violent overthrow of the Commune in 1871. Possibly the self-love, the trim, pedantic obduracy of the French middle class, owes a great deal to its roots in the satisfactions of a successful peasantry. (They got what they wanted after the Revolution and, frugally, what they have they hold.)

Again, there seems to be a Manichaean overtone in discussions about the class: the conflict is between the children of light and the children of darkness. In Genet's novels, his criminals, traitors, male prostitutes, pimps, collaborators and Nazis are known by adjectives that convey light and brightness. Those of us who close his works in anger and disgust at his sacrilege live in the outer darkness of right thinking. Hell is not an extreme; it is in the middle.

Absolutists put their money on Being rather than Action: they are after our souls. If Genet can be said to have mystical claims they are in his interest in the 'dark night' of the soul; but the soul, in Christian thought, emerges from its 'dark night'— see the lives of the saints. Genet's murderers and cheats do not emerge. They live out of drama impenetrable to others. For Genet's experiences as a thief, a reformatory boy and burglar, and one who has seen murder (but is not a murderer) have taught him—because he is a gifted man, a sort of poet and rhetorician—that criminals are a stupid, dingy lot of short-sighted morons. Their 'dark night' is really a grey night. Having opted out of society, and narrowed by their monotonous hatreds, they find their momentarily experienced liberty is a wilderness: they long for punishment in the extremely complacent society of prison in which they spend most of their lives if they survive the treacheries of their friends. (Anyone who has had a passing acquaintance with the convicted knows that many consider the wicked are outside of jail.) Genet draws portraits brilliantly in detail with all the passion and *parti pris* of prison society: he admires what can be called the *virtu* of the profession like an aesthete. A good burglar may be self-condemned, but he has pride in his superstitions, his techniques and rituals. Reform is a loss of skill. To be incurable is both a fate and a vanity. He is unknown to loyalty, mercy, pity or charity (i.e., *bonté*).

How does it come about that Genet, a writer so committed to his theme, is able to be without illusions about the criminal? A Sade sees himself as a revolutionary energy; a Dostoevsky, who can so thoroughly abandon himself, for a time, in the idea of 'beyond good and evil,' sees Christ and Salvation. Genet sees nothing. He is a total nihilist, angered by *ennui*. In a really admirable exposition, Richard N. Coe describes him as a lucid schizophrenic and makes a very convincing (and anti-Sartre case) for Genet as one living between those disparate poles that at a touch create the electric spark of poetry. Philip Thody, in a cooler but equally searching work—written, I think, in 1968—contains a little more biographical material, and suggests, if I read him aright, that Genet was a 'made' criminal and not a born one, relying on Genet's words that he became a thief because he was called a thief. It was the result of shock. And that he was able to 'cure' himself by a truly astonishing discovery of language; he entered not a moral world, but a world of words and images.

It is certainly true that his prose is very fine, and that his virtuosity as a writer is enormous: he proceeds from criminal ritual to the literary, without losing his innate interest in violence. He has a marked humour. The paradox and the ambiguity that floor the critic who tries to formulate Genet's thought are the sparks flying off from the brutal hammer-on-anvil of experience. He was born existential. His work is autobiographical but more forcefully so for anticipating the masks, the disguises, the involvement of the reader, assumed by later writers of the *nouveau roman*.

An important feature, also, is Genet's preoccupation with Things. Things exist, have a magnetism, and are as inciting as persons: the majority of his characters are homosexual, but it is the holster, the belt, the jackboot, the badge, the uniform of the

male lover that allure: the picturesque argot of buggery, its un-
ecstatic clinical detail, are themselves like objects in a 'black'
museum at police headquarters. It is true there is a passing
sexual tenderness and naïvety. Particularly in a book like
Funeral Rites—which critics think to be a falling off and which
shows an ambiguous and provocative attraction to Nazism—
one seems to be in a collector's gallery. In defence of this book
it must be said we have forgotten the seamy side of the Liberation in Paris.

The poetry of Genet's novels is fragmentary. This has a
special force, because of the abrupt and necessarily fragmentary
nature of the criminal's life: he never sees beyond his nose as he
heads toward punishment or his own death. Genet's virtuosity
lies in his management of rapid discursiveness and sudden clinch-
ing scenes, in the skill in moving back and forward in time, and in
the convincing though arbitrary way in which the author takes
himself with a sort of effrontery from the outside to the inside of
character. The defects are sudden descents into banal reflection
and in over-all pretentiousness. We are not all that far from the
idealization of the criminal. There is a theatrical suggestion—
especially in the German references, the hatred of France, and so
on—of 'the twilight of the Gods'.

And it is both the originality and the tedium of the writer
that his impulse is one of personal revenge. (There are scarcely
any women in Genet's novels and although this is due to his
homosexuality, which is passive and feminine, it has an obvious
root in his rage at being abandoned by his mother, who was a
prostitute.) The hymn of hate springs from sterility, though it
is relieved by a savage humour and by one or two remarkable
big scenes. The locale is always deeply there: I think of the eerie
seduction in the Tiergarten, or the horror of the hot stink of
shooting, fear and rape in the long rooftop scene in the Paris
street-fighting.

Genet is the natural production of an age of violence, a natural cult-figure for those who feel guilty because they have escaped martyrdom. He offers everything to the voyeur in ourselves. Sartre tried to push him into politics but except in his play *The Blacks* that has not borne results. I find the interest in the orgies of disgust in the novels, and the attempt to shock us by half-arguing for Hitler and the Nazis, monotonous as scandals. One gets in the novels something of the self-caressing dreariness and pettiness that date, I suppose, from a much better writer like Restif de la Bretonne. The lack of charity is an appalling defect and one rebels against the claustrophobia. His characteristic material is seen to my mind to far better effect in the theatre, simply because the theatre is drastic and has design. The scene in *Funeral Rites* where the drunken Nazi shoots at his Other Self in the mirror is pure theatre.

Genet's rather portentous conceit of the Self, the mirror Self and the Double, works well in the theatre and draws out his extraordinary technical skill. It emphasizes the dream or nightmare frame in which his violence is set and which establishes him as an artist as well as a pornographer. *The Maids* is as good as anything in Strindberg's theatre.

Without the aid of commentators like Thody and of Coe I do not get far with the novels. Coe warns us not to stop at the fact that Genet's novels interpret criminal psychology; he tells us to see the symbolism. This puzzles me. Genet's paradoxes and contradictions seem to be native to the poet of violence and not to a thinker. It is a good argument that Genet is a taboo breaker rather than a law-breaker.

What I got from *Funeral Rites*, after its view of the hoodlum temperament and passive homosexuality, was his capacity to evoke a really frightening sadness, the *tristesse* of the incurable. It is a novel about hatred and sex, lived by people grieving in a void or limbo. The void is all the worse for being small, a place —if that is the word—where people exist only as bodies with sexual or bullet holes in them. Coe thinks that there are signs of something more than a factitious virility in Genet's later work. It would be striking to see Genet achieving the masculine instinct for responsibility and a sense of proportion, but perhaps this would silence him as a writer. Inside his great vanity, a serious artist is clearly at grips with his conflicts.

ZOLA

Zola's Life

ZOLA STANDS IN his time, the latter half of the French nineteenth century, when the energies of industrialism and social
change throbbed, a time above all of awakened appetites for
power. Zola, as we see him from the outside, is Appette in
person, a continuous consumer. Like some powerful locomotive, he eats up facts and lives as if they were so much coal,
choking us with enormous clouds of smoke which were both
dream and nightmare. This was what his public, on which he
kept a close eye, looked for. Their lives were drab. They were
looking for dramas of escape, the satisfactions of desires which
had been repressed by the work ethic and, being the children of
'Get Rich' Guizot and his educational reforms, they were new
to literacy and a little leisure. The scientific pretensions of Zola's
Naturalism, his social concern and his half-poetic violence and
melodrama, were exactly their meat.

Professor Hemmings's *Life* is the first biography in English
for twenty-five years. He has collated the new material now
available to scholars and his book is a thoughtful, inquiring and
well-written book and commands a very necessary perspective.
It puts the light and shade on a complex character whom we
had seen only in black and white.

Professor Hemmings's first point is that Zola was a sensational
artist in a century which had turned to the novel for its emotions
and instruction very much in the way our own mass public
turns to the cinema, television and radio. The novel was the
medium. Like Dickens of an earlier generation, he went after
his public. He was an excellent storyteller with a strong sense of

fatality. The mills of Reason grind more dramatically than the mills of God: the fantasies of Zola depend on documentation and a deep concern for Truth and Justice. There *are* comic passages in Zola's novels, but our main impression is of the efficient pistons of the locomotive's seriousness. Yet, *L'Assommoir* (The Dram Shop), *La Terre* (The Land) and *Germinal* are probably great novels, the *Thérèse Raquin* is the work of an unflinching moralist. What can be held against him is that his subjects become vaguer as they become larger and larger at the end of his career.

Professor Hemmings is careful to see Zola's sensationalism against the background of his passionate liberal beliefs; Zola was no intellectual but he was the bitter enemy of authoritarianism, obscurantism and racial prejudice; he was the forceful man of reason who believed absolutely in the benefits of science; he can be called 'a true heir of the *encyclopédistes* of the eighteenth century. . . . He sought to consolidate the achievements of the Enlightenment.' Truth and Justice are his slogans.

But unlike the immensely marketable believer, the man is not all of a piece. Like Balzac, his exemplar, he was an almost perpetual worker, mostly seen grinding at his desk, a fat, sedentary, myopic figure. Unlike Balzac he lacks magnetism; he is even dull, respectable, shy and personally humourless. He certainly makes no attempt to live out his fantasies as Balzac so ruinously did, though he did keep a considerable tonnage of absurd bric-à-brac in the famous house at Médan. Late in middle age, when he broke his long fidelity to his childless wife and took a peasant girl as his mistress, we do indeed see a repressed Zola appear; even so, there is something dogged and planned about the passion. Overeating had made him (and his wife) gross and hypochondriacal; when he was considering the possibility of love for a young girl, he saw he must prepare for the contingency by going on a diet. As thorough here in self-documentation as he was in his career, he undertook this.

What had Zola repressed? When we turn to the account of Zola's remarkable and far more attractive father, we can see what haunted the novelist. Zola *père* was a Venetian of distinguished family, a brilliant, amorous and adventurous mining engineer and a pioneer among the builders of European railways. Heads of governments listened to him. He was far-seeing and practical, but, at the last moment, men more gifted in raising capital either diddled him or took over his work. In early middle age, he died poor in Aix, where he had married a working-class French woman and thereby established his son's kinship with the common people. The son's emotional capital and capacity for living, one would say, had been exhausted by his gifted father, who left him, however, his respect for work and the imaginative intelligence. (One curious connection with his father's life and career as an engineer can be seen in the peculiar dream of tunneling in *Germinal*.) Literature would be the young Zola's science and industry; his knowledge of working-class poverty and the desire to get out of it were the spur. His sexual temperature was low. His emotions would be absorbed by his simple mother first and then by the able and maternal mistress who became his wife. She also had had to make her own way as an illegitimate child and is thought to have been a florist.

It is a surprise to find that the vigorous, astute and apparently very masculine Zola was a frail and sickly, even rather feminine, young man shut in by anxieties. The violent interest in sex and the lusts of the flesh which give a carnal vividness to his novels was the fantasy of a shy man—it seems—of small performance. His continence in a free-living period was a popular joke among French cartoonists. His imagination was sensual to the point of being pornographic; his life was blameless. Men who have known hunger when they were young are likely to become gluttonous later on, and one can see why an imaginative greed and a dramatic sense of all human hungers appear in his novels:

a greed for sex, fame, money and success, for huge novels that are like enormous highly spiced meals. In one of his famous crowd scenes in *Germinal*, the people are described in terms of their hungry mouths. In *L'Assommoir* the mouth is the drinker's mouth. In these scenes there is gaudy poetry which is also visionary.

The visions have—when we turn to his life—a double source. One can trace this first to his early childhood in Aix where he was a happy and intelligent boy until his spirited Italian father died; secondly to the serious, dreaming, hopeful friendship with the young Cézanne when they talked about their genius as they went swimming. (Zola was at this time a better painter than Cézanne.) After the father's death and the family's move to Paris, the struggle against extreme poverty began. The young Zola slaving in a bookshop felt the iron sense of responsibility for the family. This experience and the haunting friendship with Cézanne—their common feeling of the dream of art—formed him. Cézanne was determined on solitude; Zola was cut out for action and publicity. About the latter he was shameless and pushing; when he was savagely attacked he collected the libels as a sort of treasury or capital. The greater feeder chewed them over: they added to his energies.

Professor Hemmings is especially suggestive on the subject of Zola and the Impressionists. One can see how important they were to him, of course, from *L'Oeuvre*, in which Cézanne is one of his models and in the end theatrically dramatized. One can see what the attraction was; the Impressionists too practised a scientific Naturalism in their manner. They were also in revolt against authority; and Zola was the man for a cause. He was fighting for his career and their careers. He knew what poverty and obloquy were. When in middle life he turned against Cézanne it was because Cézanne had not succeeded. At the height of his own career Zola could only pity failure—and perhaps feared failure himself. All this is evident from the correspondence between the two men.

Far more interesting is another suggestion: Mr Hemmings ponders the question of Zola's bad eyesight. A curious personal vanity made him refuse to wear glasses until late in life, and the suggestion is that his poor vision may have prevented him from really *seeing* the pictures of the Impressionists; their prismatic light was created by the accumulation of immense detail which, to Zola, would appear as a vague general mist, dreamlike at first, ultimately muddy. Is this the reason for the vagueness in Zola's crowd scenes, his large-scale images and his poster-like symbolism? On the other hand, vagueness in these painters would come to suggest weakness of purpose and lack of social direction to which Zola the storyteller and social moralist was emphatically hostile. Except for its brilliant account of the crowd at the Salon, *L'Oeuvre* is a naïvely divided book in which Sandoz-Zola presents himself as the truly great artist—successful, responsible, toiling, suffering the agonies of creation: Lantier-Cézanne is the *raté*, who in a preposterous scene which perhaps discloses the hysteria buried in Zola's life is raped by his own wife, renounces his art, destroys his last picture and hangs himself.

It is common for writers, indeed all artists, to sink into depression when they have finished a work, but it is strange that Zola's pessimism at this time took the form of a fantasy of violence and self-destruction. When the man who scarcely left his desk began his liaison with the gentle seamstress his wife had taken into the bourgeois mansion, his guilt once more led to fears of violence. He was convinced that his wife would murder the girl and the two children she bore. Perhaps the idea was, as we would say, very Italian; his imagination perhaps craved the operatic. In prosaic fact, after frightful scenes, the wife refused divorce for she did not want to throw away her status as the partner of a famous man, and was peaceably won over by the children. She had none of her own.

It is so much in character that Zola, the prophet of modernity and Naturalism, should have been taken by the craze for photography and, before the affair began, used the seamstress as his first model. His preparation via slimming now received the stimulus of a new form of documentation. Yet as Professor Hemmings says, the very nervousness and solicitude with which he approached the young girl were aspects of his solemn decency. His tenderness for human circumstance is the sign of a serious moral nature. If the theme of the guilty secret now appears in his later works, that simply shows that the great novelists have always used every bit of themselves. His guilt enhances his respectability and when we look between the excesses of his novels we see how moving and true he is about the consolations and responsibilities of everyday life in its work and its humble pleasures. When Madame Zola took an interest in his mistress's children, her husband wrote affectionate letters to her telling her what the children were doing and how once he had tested the little girl on her scripture lessons! Professor Hemmings writes:

It is hard to decide which is stranger: that Zola should have kept his lawful wife informed about the activities of his children by another woman, or that this obdurate freethinker should have displayed such solicitude for their religious education. In a novel he would never have permitted himself such paradoxes. . . .

His melodramas came from another self.

Zola's intervention in the Dreyfus affair—he did not meet Dreyfus until it was all over and found him dim and disappointing—might seem to have a theatrical and even self-publicizing motive. In fact *J'Accuse* was the most disinterested act of Zola' life. It brought him great popular abuse and indeed exile. Stronger even than his hatred of anti-Semitism was his loathing of corrupt authority, the covering up by professional groups, the tricks of the High Command, the judges, the politicians and a self-serving bureaucracy. Zola was unbendable in his stand for truth-telling and the principles of the law. His tenacity is amazing. He acted as a citizen, not as a novelist, and stood firm against the considerable mass of people who were opposed to him. There is a story that when years later he died of asphyxiation caused by the fumes from the stove in his study, an anti-Semitic workman confessed to having closed the ventilator in the chimney as an act of revenge. The tale has never been confirmed; it sounds too Zola-esque to be true, but it is certainly possible.

George Sand

THE SPELL IMPOSED by George Sand on European and Russian readers and critics in the nineteenth century is understandable; her people and landscapes are silhouettes seen in streams of sheet lightning. For ourselves, what has been left is her notorious life story and the throbbing of her powerful temperament. Yet Balzac, Dostoevsky and—of all people—Matthew Arnold admired her as a novelist. Proust admired her sinuous and gliding prose and Flaubert her exotic imagination. There she was pouring out ink in her sixty novels, her enormous autobiography, her works of travel and her thousands of letters; a thinking bosom and one who overpowered her young lovers; all sybil, teacher, a Romantic, and, in the end, a respectable Victorian moralist.

There were hostile voices of course. As Curtis Cate reminds us in his exhaustive biography published four years ago, Baudelaire burst out with an attack on what had most allured her admirers:

> She has always been a moralist. Only, previously she had indulged in anti-morality. She has thus never been an artist. She has the famous flowing style dear to the bourgeois. She is stupid, she is ponderous, she is long-winded: she has in moral judgments the same depth of judgment and the same delicacy of feeling as concierges and kept women.

(These last two words are wildly wrong: one thing she certainly was not was a pampered courtesan. She spent the large sums of money she earned extravagantly and a large part in charity.)

Shuddering at her candour Henry James was closer to her in his judgement on her talents. Her novels, he said, had turned faint,

> as if the image projected, not intense, not absolutely concrete— failed to reach completely the mind's eye. . . . The wonderful change of expression is not really a remedy for the lack of intensity, but rather an aggravation of it through a sort of suffusion of the whole thing by the voice and speech of the author. . . . [There is] a little too much of the feeling of going up in a balloon. We are borne by a fresh cool current and the car delightfully dangles, but as we peep over the sides we see things—as we usually know them—at a dreadful drop beneath.

The woman who was known for her gifts as a silent listener took to the upper air when she shut herself up at night and became garrulous in ink.

Now, it is evident, an attempt to draw the general reader back to George Sand is underway. The most obvious reason for this is opportunism of the women's liberation kind, where she is bound to be a disappointment to those who look for a guru. A disconcerting sybil she may have been; as a priestess she hedged. The Saint-Simonians were discouraged when they tried to turn her into the Mrs Eddy of free love. A more interesting lure to contemporary taste is suggested by Diane Johnson in her introduction to the novelist's edifying Gothic romance, *Mauprat*, written in the 1830s. Mrs Johnson says that if George Sand's temperament was too strong for her writing, temperament was her subject as an artist:

> . . . readers have come to hold in new high regard the truths of the imagination, the romantic principle, the idea that the passionate artist had access to truths and secrets of human nature more interesting than mere dramas of social arrival.

Gothic melodrama is back with us, if in dank condition, 'for reasons best understood today in terms of psychology, but understood very well by George Sand in universal terms.' (The universal is the trouble.) It is true, at any rate, that the Romantics—especially those of the second wave, the *Hernani* generation—set the artist apart as the supreme seer in society; and that for all their extravagance of feeling and even because of it, they were excellent pre-Freudian psychologists. Their very violence is a prediction and their inflation of the ballooning self makes it dramatic and macroscopic. We have to add that she is shamelessly autobiographical. The love affair of the week, month or year, along with mysticism, socialism and The People was transposed into the novel that promptly followed; she spoke of herself as 'the consumer' of men and women too, and the men often turned out to be projections of herself. The passions of her characters, their powerful jealousies, their alternations of exaltation and gloom, were her own. She was half Literature.

Her finer powers emerged when her fame as a novelist declined, above all in her *Histoire de ma vie*, in her lively travel writing and her letters. In her letters there is no need of Gothic castles or dreadful ravines: her mundane experience was extraordinary enough in itself. As a traveller she had eyes, ears and verve. The short pastoral novels *La mare au diable* (*The Haunted Pool*) or *François le Champi* (*The Country Waif*) are serene masterpieces drawn from her childhood and her love of nature, which awakened her senses as they awakened Colette's. She was close to the peasants of Nohant. The self is in these tales, but it is recollected or transposed in tranquility—in her own early life she had known what it was to be a waif, albeit a very fortunate one. These works have never lost their quiet, simple, truth-telling power and we understand why Turgenev, Henry James, and, later, Malraux praised them.

George Sand was the child of one of Napoleon's well-born officers. He was a descendant of the great Maréchal de Saxe and therefore, on the wrong side of the blanket, of the King of Poland. Her mother was a plebeian woman, the hot-tempered daughter of a Paris innkeeper and bird fancier. The inner class conflict enriched both George Sand's exuberant imagination and those sympathies with the poor which took her into radical politics; strangely like Tolstoy—but without his guilt or torment—she turned to presenting the peasantry not as quaint folk or a gospel, but as sentient, expressive beings. She listened to the curious Berrichon dialect and translated it, without folkish affectations or condescensions, into a truthful expression of plain human feeling. She had the humility and concern to discard dramatic earnestness without losing her psychological acumen or her art as a story teller who keeps her people in focus as the tradition of Pastoral does: very often her best work is a gloss on traditional forms.

In the feminist foreground of the present revival is *Lélia*, the confessional novel which she wrote at the age of twenty-nine in 1833 after the rebellion against her marriage, the break with Jules Sandeau, and the disastrous attempts to obtain sexual pleasure from an expert like Mérimée, or from any other man as far as we know. Chopin said she loved extremely but was incapable of making love. Partly because of its attacks on the Church and the marriage system, the male hold on property and the double standard, partly because of its erotic revelation and the rumour of a lesbian attachment to the actress Marie Dorval, the book itself was attacked for outrageous and morbid candour. Lélia is intended to be a Romantic heroine, a doomed but indomitable soul, one pursuing a mystical quest for spiritual love. She is beautiful, intellectual, independent, yet tormented by a sensuality that is nevertheless incapable of sexual happiness. She cannot be a nun like Santa Teresa nor can she be a courtesan or married woman. The dreams of a poetically exalted adolescence have divorced the heart from the body. Literature has paralyzed her. She says of a lover:

When I was near him I felt a sort of strange and delirious greed which, taking its source from the keenest powers of my intelligence, could not be satisfied by any carnal embrace. I felt my bosom devoured by an inextinguishable fire, and his kisses shed no relief. I pressed him in my arms with a superhuman force, and fell next to him exhausted, discouraged at having no possible way to convey to him my passion. With me desire was an ardour of the soul that paralyzed the power of the senses before it awakened them. It was a savage fury that seized my brain and concentrated itself there exclusively. My blood froze, impotent and poor, before the immense soaring of my will . . .

When he was drowsy, satisfied, and at rest, I would lie motionless beside him. I passed many hours watching him sleep. He seemed so handsome to me! There was so much force and grandeur on his peaceful brow. Next to him my heart palpitated violently. Waves of blood mounted to my face. Then unbearable tremblings passed through my limbs. I seemed to experience again the excitation of physical love and the increasing turmoil of desire. I was violently tempted to awaken him, to hold him in my arms, and to ask for his caresses from which I hadn't yet known how to profit. But I resisted these deceiving entreaties of my suffering because I well knew it wasn't in his power to calm me.

The stone images of Catholic 'palaces of worship' give no comfort, for her imagination responds chiefly to the figurations of medieval nightmare: scaly serpents, hideous lizards, agonized chimeras and emblems of sin, illusion and suffering. Sublimation has two faces:

When the red rays of the setting sun played on their forms, I seemed to see their flanks swell, their spiny fins dilate, their faces contract into new tortures. . . . While I contemplated these bodies engulfed in masses of stone, which the hand of neither man nor time had been able to dislodge, I identified myself with these images of eternal struggle between suffering and necessity, between rage and impotence.

The nightmares of the unconscious haunt the aspirant. And

we are warned that when spring comes to stir the senses, all attempt to deny the calyx or the bud, by the study of botany, or to turn to science, will not annul the ferment of the imagination. As always in George Sand, poetic observation and imagery is rather fine: but the inevitable tutorial follows.

I take these passages from Maria Espinosa's translation. She has worked on the 1833 edition which George Sand toned down three years later. This early edition has not been done into English until now, and the version is remarkable for coming very close to the resonant vocabulary and its extraordinary physical images. If there is a loss it is because English easily droops into a near-evangelical tune; our language is not made for operatic precisions and we have a limited tradition of authorized hyperbole. Abstractions lose the intellectual formality that has an exact ring in French.

It is important to remember, also, that George Sand's prose feeds on a sensibility to music which dated from her childhood: she was alert to all sounds in nature and to all delicacies and sonorities of voice and instrument. (Her novels might be described as irresistible overtures to improbable operas which are —as they proceed—disordered by her didactic compulsion.) *Lélia*, I think, rises above this, because it is so personal and arbitrary in its succession of sounds and voices, and we are bounced into accepting the hyperbole as we would be if it were sung, though we may be secretly bored by the prolonging of the moans.

In *Lélia* we listen to five voices: there is the voice of Sténio, the young poet lover whom Lélia freezes with Platonic love: she is an exalted *allumeuse*; there is Trenmor, the elderly penitent gambler and stoic—her analysis of the gambler's temperament is the best thing in the book: George Sand was at heart a gambler—there is Magnus, the fanatic priest who is made mad by the suppression of his sexual desires and who sees Lélia as a she-devil; there is Pulchérie, Lélia's sister, a genial courtesan living for sexual pleasure; and Lélia herself, defeated by her sexual coldness, horrified by the marriage bed, the mocker of a stagnant society, religion and the flesh. She is sick with self-love and her desires approach the incestuous: she seeks weak men who cannot master her, to whom she can be either a dominating mother, sister or nurse.

In chorus these voices sing out the arguments for and against spiritual love. As in opera, the plot is preposterous and scenes are extravagant and end without warning. Pulchérie introduces a pagan and worldly note and also—it must be said—the relief of more than a touch of nature. She reminds the miserable Lélia of a charming incident in their childhood when the beauty of Lélia troubled her as they lay sleeping on the mossy bank dear to Romantic fiction. Pulchérie says:

Your thick, black hair clung to your face, and the close curls tightened as if a feeling of life had clenched them next to your neck, which was velvet with shadow and sweat. I passed my fingers through your hair. It seemed to squeeze and draw me toward you. . . . In all your features, in your position, in your appearance, which was more rigid than mine, in the deeper tint of your complexion, and especially in that fierce, cold expression on your face as you slept, there was something masculine and strong which nearly prevented me from recognizing you. I found that you resembled the handsome young man with the black hair of whom I had just dreamed. Trembling, I kissed your arm. Then you opened your eyes, and your gaze penetrated me with shame. . . . But, Lélia, no impure thought had even presented itself to me. How had it happened? I knew nothing. I received from nature and from God my first lesson in love, my first sensation of desire.

The scenes of Lélia's despair take place inevitably in an abandoned monastery, with its debris that suggest the horrors of death and the futility of existence. Lélia says:

At times I tried to find release by crying out my suffering and anger. The birds of the night flew away terrified or answered me with savage wailings.

(Nature always responds to George Sand.)

The noise echoed from vault to vault, breaking against those shaky ruins; and the gravel that slid from the rooftops seemed to presage the fall of the edifice on my head.

That gravel, it must be said, is excellent observation. Her comment is typically orchestral:

Oh, I would have wished it were so! I redoubled my cries, and those walls echoed my voice with a more terrible and heart-rending sound. They [the ruins] seemed inhabited by legions of the damned, eager to respond and unite with me in blasphemy.

These terrible nights were followed by days of bleak stupor.

A scene of Oriental luxury was indispensable to the Romantics: the looting of Egypt was Napoleon's great gift to literature. There is the fantastic ball given by Prince Bambuccj in which lovers can disappear into boudoirs and artificial caves as busily as bees. The trumpets, one must say, acclaim the triumphs of fornication; they are gorgeously brazen in the lascivious scene; the perfumes are insidious. Pulchérie and Lélia are masked and Lélia plots to pass off Pulchérie as herself so that Sténio is deceived into thinking his cold mistress has relented. He awakens and is shattered by the deceit. He stands at the window of the palace and hears the voice of Lélia mocking him—in a somewhat classy way—from a pretty boat that floats by in the Asiatic lagoon. This is an operatic scene of a high order. Calamity, of course. Having tasted flesh, Sténio becomes a drunken debauchee and eventually commits suicide. If he starts, in real life, as the innocent Jules Sandeau, he ends as the drunken

Musset. Magnus, the mad priest, is now sure that Lélia is possessed by a devil and strangles her. With a rosary, of course. One recalls that Lélia has had fantasies of strangulation.

Lélia is one of those self-dramatizations that break off as mood follows mood. She asks what God intended for men and women: whether he intended them to meet briefly and leave each other at once, for otherwise the sexes would destroy each other; whether the hypocrisy of a bourgeois society is the enemy; whether intellectual vision must be abnormal; whether poetry and religion corrupt. All the voices are George Sand herself—and very aware, as she frankly said, that she belonged to a generation which, for the moment, was consciously out to shock. What she did not expect was laughter. She had little sense of humour.

One can see how much of the book comes out of Hoffmann and even more precisely from Balzac's equally chaotic and melodramatic *La Peau de chagrin*. Lélia, it has often been noted, is the female Raphael de Valentin. Both writers feel the expanding energies of the new century; both have the confident impulse toward the Absolute and to Omniscience; but hers is the kind of imagination and intellect that breaks off before suggesting a whole. Balzac and Sand were both absorbed by an imaginative greed; they worked themselves to the bone, partly because they were like that, partly because they created debts and openly sought a vast public. Their rhetoric was a nostalgia for the lost Napoleonic glory.

How thoroughly she toiled in her social-problem novels! The tedious *Compagnon du Tour de France* is a garrulous study of the early trade unions, a politically pious book, enlivened by her strong visual sense. In the far more sympathetic *Mauprat* she goes to the heart of her life-long debt to Rousseau: the young brutal Mauprat who belongs to the brigand and mafioso branch of an aristocratic family rescues the aristocratic heroine from his gang—but with the intention of raping her on the quiet. She frustrates the attempt and is shown redeeming her brute: to love he must pass through a long psychological re-education. This is achieved but not entirely in a sentimental way; both he and the women are hot-tempered, sulky and sensitive to points of honour.

George Sand herself did not think we should be punished for our sins or our grave faults of character, but that we were called upon to learn from them: they were—*grace à* Rousseau—opportunities for interesting self-education and reform. She is not a doctrinaire like Gorki in his communist phase. Her advantage as a woman is that she is a psychologist who gives hostilities their emotional due: they are indications of the individual's right to his temperament. She may have been a domineering, ruthless woman and very cunning and double-minded with it, but there is scarcely a book that is not redeemed by her perceptions, small though they may be.

She understands the rich very well—'There are hours of impunity in château life'—and she thinks of the poor as individuals but flinches from them as a case. Two words recur continually in her works: 'delirium,' which may be ecstatic, bad, or, more interestingly, a psychological outlet; and 'boredom'—energy and desire had been exhausted. One can see that she is woman but not Woman. The little fable of *François de Champi* shows that she used every minute of her life; for not only was she in a fortunate sense a waif, as I have said, but an enlightened waif; and we note that when François grows up he marries the widow who has been a mother to him. Most of George Sand's men were waifs in one way or another; the Higher Incest was to be their salvation. Women were the real power figures, whereas men were consumable. She liked to pilfer their brains.

She certainly sought only gifted men who were usually sick and with whom she could assume the more powerful role of mother and nurse. Chopin was her 'child'. Sandeau was her 'little brother'. What about Michel de Bourges, her proletarian lawyer and Christian Communist, who almost converted her to the need for violent revolution and the guillotine? Here was a virile man, and he could offer oratory, notoriety, and powerful embraces, but he was in bad health, too; she became frenzied —but was it the frenzy she desired? It may have been. She defiantly walked the streets of his native town in trousers and smoking her pipe, enjoyed the scandal, and caused scenes between him, his wife and his fat mistress. He was a tyrant, and one might think this was what she sought. Not at all. *She* could not dominate *him*; despite her passion for him, which drove her to ride for miles at night for a short, Chatterley-like tryst, he could not subdue the strongest thing in her—her intellect.

Michel de Bourges was responsible for her wordy novels of social revolt, but he could not break her opposition to the utilitarian view of art. Like all the Romantics, she believed in the vision of the artist as the unique and decisive spiritual force in society. He might dismiss all this as a self-regarding bourgeois delusion, but she would not yield. All the same, she wrote propaganda for the republican cause in '48, and when the reaction came she handed out money to the hunted proletarian poets and took advantage of acquaintance with Louis Napoleon to get her friends and fellow-writers out of jail. In Nohant, she was a scandal because of her lovers. The villagers imagined orgies when the young men came and went. After '48, she was a political scandal. The obsequious villagers touched their caps but sneered behind her back. This did not disturb her. She was a country girl at heart and knew that revolution was an urban industrial notion; in the countryside it meant nothing. And, in fact, the country crowd, particularly the women, took her side when the husband she had deserted made two savage and incompetent efforts in court to get Nohant from her.

This episode is thoroughly gone into by Mr Cate. It is important, for it brings out where she stood—or wobbled—on the crucial question of marriage and free love. The two court actions have the inevitable air of comedy: Michel de Bourges was her lover and her advocate, yet she had to appear respectable and demure. No trousers and no pipe now; she appeared in shawl and bonnet. An absurd but useful opportunity occurred for her to ascend astutely into the upper air when questions of adultery and free love were brought up. Those exalted ladies of the Saint-Simonian persuasion came to address her as a priestess. They invited her to become a 'mother' of the Saint-Simonian 'family', or phalanstery, and even sent a load of hand-made presents, which included shoes, trousers, waistcoats, collars, one watercolour and a riding crop. In reply, she recommended them to practice the ancient morality of faithful marriage for 'being the most difficult, [it] is certainly the finest', though she would not blame those who shook themselves free of tyranny, which was the product of a false society. The fact is that for her, as for her fellow-Romantics, the just society already existed metaphysically, and that in this sense she was chaste. And she was no fool. She *was* temporarily chaste with her lawyer, but at home, at Nohant, she kept another pretender, whom she was maddening with the kisses of platonic affection. This was Charles Didier, a Genevan, and Mr Cate differs from André Maurois' judgement in his opinion of his character. How far they went, no one knows; to judge by his tortured 'Journal', Didier himself seems unsure. All he could report was hugs that seem maternal. It is nearly impossible to translate the language of the Romantics, but in reply to one of his injured letters George Sands is masterly. She could easily squash rancour:

You don't love, all I can do is love. Friendship for you is a contract with clauses for the well-combined advantage of both parties, for me it is sympathy, embrace, identity, it is the complete adoption of the qualities and faults of the person one feels to be one's friend. . . . You attribute to me . . . a calculated dryness, how shall I put it?—something worse, a kind of prostitution of the heart, full of baseness, egotism, falseness, you make me out to be a kind of platonic slut. . . . My misfortune is to throw myself wholeheartedly at each fine soul I encounter. . . . What I took for a noble soul is a gloomy, sickly suspicious soul that has lost the ability to believe and thus to love.

Honesty or sophistry? Goodness knows. Better to call it incantation. Didier was soon forgotten. The loss of Michel de Bourges looked fatal to her reason, but she was quickly, so to say, back in the saddle. An amusing actor arrived, and there was soon a troupe of young men, all hoping to be the favourite.

And, distributing her kisses, back to her room she went for her nightly five- or six-hour stint on the next novel. The blood —her own and that of others—was turned into ink. We remember the cold words of Solange, the daughter who was no less wilful than herself: 'It would take a shrewd fellow to unravel the character of my mother.'

FLAUBERT

The Quotidian

ALTHOUGH MARRED BY affectations of style, Professor Brombert's study of the themes and techniques of Flaubert's novels is a full and very suggestive scrutiny of Flaubert's love-hate of realism, as it is woven into the texture of his narratives. Flaubert's own ambiguities on the subject are clear. 'I abhor what has been called realism, although they make me out to be one of its high priests,' he wrote to George Sand. He hated reality. (Or rather it disgusted him; that is also an attraction.) Art held priority over life. If so much of his work is minutely drawn from everyday life, he forced himself to depict it (in Professor Brombert's words):

> partly out of self-imposed therapy to cure himself of his chronic idealism, partly also out of a strange and almost morbid fascination. . . . Art for him was quite literally an escape . . . For hatred of reality . . . was intimately bound up with an inherent pessimism—and pessimism in turn was one of the prime conditions of his ceaseless quest for ideal forms.

In resilient moments he called himself an old '*romantique enragé*': even, a *troubadour*.

All this is well known; we know an enormous amount about Flaubert and Professor Brombert brings all the important critics into his net. But, a good deal owing to Marxist and Christian criticism, the quite gratuitous notion has got about that Flaubert was not what he ought to have been. He ought not to have been 'an alienated bourgeois'; yet, surely, a vast number of great artists have been 'alienated' from their dispensation and especially in the ninteenth century. Alienation is a cant term for a necessary condition. The 'hatred' of Balzac, Stendhal, Zola, Flaubert or Proust are the characteristic engines of a century bemused by its own chaotic energies. The force of criticism from an outside position of Marxist, Christian or psychoanalytical neo-conformity is now fading and one is at least heartened to see Professor Brombert applying himself to 'the unique temperament and vision that determine and characterize a novelist's work as we find them in the text'.

There can be two weaknesses in this kind of criticism; first it puritanically denies side glances at biography, social influences, etc., and rather hypocritically assumes that we have had these necessities privately at the back door. Professor Brombert is not too strict here; how could one leave out the effect of atheistic medical observation and the morgue on Flaubert's mind? Even Flaubert's obsession with style seems to have something of medical specialization in it. Secondly, the critic may find too much in the text and build top-heavy theories on images and symbols, as one finds, for example, when this kind of criticism deals with Dickens: all that talk of baptismal water! (I have only one doubt about Professor Brombert's attention to key words: this is when he catalogues the symbols of liquefaction.)

In Flaubert the danger is usually small for he was the most conscious of artists; a most ardent collector of echoes and symbols. His documentary interest in *things* is also a concern with what they tell of the imagination. Things are corrupted or corrupting. He is tortured by the fact that the century has turned mind into matter, the ideal converted into ludicrous or detestable paraphernalia.

Take the matter of the Algerian scarves in *Madame Bovary*. They were coming into fashion with the beginning of French colonisation of North Africa: that is a comment both on bourgeois enterprise and greed, and on the absurdities of provincial taste. It is nearly a comment on the economy of the textile city of Rouen. The nineteenth century will colonize; so, in its fantasies, did the nineteenth century soul. When Emma turns spendthrift and buys curtains, carpets and hangings from the draper, the information takes on something from the theme of the novel itself: the material is a symbol of the exotic, and the exotic feeds the Romantic appetite. It will lead to satiety, bankruptcy and eventually to nihilism and the final drive towards death and nothingness.

If anyone makes too much of his images, it will be Flaubert himself: for example, the snake, in the snake-like hiss of Madame Bovary's corset lace. It is a melodramatic excess, as one can tell by the eagerness with which the image was seized upon by the lurid and falsifying mind of the prosecuting lawyer when Flaubert was being charged with obscenity. The phrase could well have gone into the *Dictionnaire des idées reçues*. Flaubert's subject is the imagination and particularly of the orgiastic adolescent kind which he never outgrew and which received almost operatic support from an early reading of the Marquis de Sade and the early extremes of the Romantic movement.

How is it that—as it seems to us now—a whole century became adolescent? Is prolonged adolescence characteristic of a new class coming to power? This is not Professor Brombert's interest; but casting an eye on the ominous *Intimate Notebooks 1840–1841*—written when Flaubert was eighteen and already pretending to be twenty—and proceeding through the novels, Professor Brombert is able to show how, exhaustively and like an infected pathologist Flaubert presented the hunger for the future, the course of ardent longings and violent desires that rise from the sensual, the horrible, and the sadistic. They turn into the virginal and mystical, only to become numbed by satiety. At this point pathological boredom leads to a final desire for death and nothingness—the Romantic syndrome. The *Notebooks* contain eager cries on behalf of adolescent bi-sexuality;

moralize on the ecstatic yet soon-to-be ashy joys of narcissism; pass, without pause, into dreams of exotic travel:

> Often I am in India, in the shade of banana trees, sitting on mats: bayaderes are dancing, swans are fluffing out their feathers on blue lakes, nature throbs with love.

One is struck by the drunken accomplishment of the young diarist, particularly by the precision and clarity of his ingenious self-study at a time of life when one is most likely to be turgid and blind. The son of Dr Flaubert has made notes which a psychiatrist would find useful. How perceptive to write, at that age:

> Sensual pleasure is pleased with itself: it relishes itself, like melancholy—both of them solitary enjoyments. . . .

The style has already the élan and excessive conviction which are the startling qualities of his first novel *November*, unpublished in his lifetime. Luckily it has in Frank Jellinek a translator who responded to the youthful yet (again) accomplished puerilities of the writer. This book, above all, contains the emotional source of *Madame Bovary*; it states the imaginative condition of romantic love, underlines the onanism at the heart of the fantasy of the virgin whore. The very absurdities of this first novel are moving, not only because of the afflatus but because of the fidelity to the course of an emotion that may be extravagant but is precisely recognizable. What astonishes is Flaubert's understanding of his experience at that age. Here he begins his career as the doctor who proceeds to diagnosis by catching the patient's fever first.

We meet one or two of the famous Flaubert obsessions: 'There was one word which seemed to me the most beautiful of all human words: "adultery" '; his horror of begetting a child; and passages like:

Since I did not use existence, existence used me: my dreams wearied me more than great labours. A whole creation, motionless, unrevealed to itself, lived mute below my life: I was a sleeping chaos of a thousand fertile elements which knew not how to manifest themselves nor what to be, still seeking their form and awaiting their mould.

As Professor Brombert says, *November* is indispensable to an understanding of *Madame Bovary*, where 'the thousand fertile elements' manifested themselves in the facts of Normandy life. Life is a dream, life is bad art; only Art, the supreme reverie can redeem it: Flaubert's pessimism is clinical and absolute. Or is it? Keeping close to the text, Professor Brombert tries to make a path through Flaubert's ingenuities, duplicities and double meanings; and taking a tip from Flaubert's own phrase that it is stupid to come to conclusions, he points out that Flaubert's pessimism is, at any rate, resilient. Style may not save us but it is a force.

There are many good things in the discussion of *Madame Bovary*. It is a novel as complex as the second part of *Don Quixote*: we shall never get to the bottom of it. For example, there is the question of how Flaubert's lyrical intention was to consort with the banal, especially in the matter of speech. In fact Flaubert's impersonality was a fraud: he contrived—since the book was a work of self-discovery and confession—all kinds of intrusion. Often openly:

. . . it is a grave mistake not to seek candour behind worn-out language, as though fullness of soul did not at times overflow in the emptiest metaphors.

And Professor Brombert comments:

This feeling that human speech cannot possibly cope with our dreams and our grief goes a long way toward explaining why so often, in the work of Flaubert, the reader has the disconcerting impression that the language of banality is caricatured and at the same time transmuted into poetry.

(Yes: the comic is poetry inverted. The effect of pure comedy is poetic.)

Flaubert has the power of transmuting the trivial. He wrote:

> My book will have the ability to walk straight on a hair, suspended between the double abyss of lyricism and vulgarity.

As Professor Brombert says, one misses the charity, the 'imperceptible human tremors' in Flaubert: there is a rift between the sophistication of the author and the confusion of the characters: but it is the test of a great writer that he can turn his dilemmas to effect. Flaubert disguises the rift by

> The telescoping of two unrelated perspectives which bestows upon the novel a unique beauty. A stereoscopic vision accounts in large part for the peculiar poetry and complexity of *Madame Bovary*.

On the subject of the death of Madame Bovary there have been wearying differences of opinion. To some she has been hounded. To others she is a silly and disreputable nonentity, her shame not worth the expense of spirit. To D. H. Lawrence she was crushed by the intellectual skill that had created her: to others no more than a cold exercise. Yet again, she has been used by Flaubert to cure himself of his own disease. In fact, as Professor Brombert shows, the theme and even something of the plot had been known to Flaubert since his youth. There are no exercises in literature. I was struck when I last read the novel —as Professor Brombert was—by the extent of the sympathy with which she is treated. She has, even when she is mocked, the honesty of an energy. Her periods of depravity do not single her out as an exceptionally deplorable being, but rather make her part of the general, glum strangeness of the people around her. She belongs to Rouen: she is what belonging to a place or a culture may mean. She is dignified by a real fate—not by the false word 'Fate', one of the clichés Flaubert derided. Delusion itself dignifies her. The comparison with *Don Quixote* imposes itself: we see

> ... her terrible isolation, her unquenchable aspiration for some unattainable ideal. Hers are dreams that destroy. But this destructive power is also their beauty, just as Emma's greatness (the word is inappropriate to literal-minded readers) is her ability to generate such dreams ... at the moment of her complete defeat in the face of reality, she acquires dignity, and even majesty.

And despite the clinical attentions of Flaubert, her fellow adolescent, I can see no force in the criticism that, in drawing her, Flaubert tried to turn himself into a woman: it may be that in putting masculinity into her—as Baudelaire said—Flaubert made her perverse. But perversity is a normal sexual ingredient as well as an article in the Romantic canon. The Romantics were good psychologists.

Professor Brombert's final remarks are new. There is an apparent negation of tragic values in Flaubert! Does he suggest a new form of tragedy, the tragedy of the very absence of Tragedy, a condition familiar to contemporary writers? There is a link between him and ourselves.

> The oppressive heterogeneity of phenomena, the fragmented immediacy of experience, the constant fading or alteration of forms. . . .

These are twentieth-century assumptions. Equally important, Flaubert diagnoses the crisis of language.

> The breakdown of language under the degrading impact of

journalism, advertisement and political slogans parallels the breakdown of a culture over-inflated with unassimilable data.

It leads to the incoherence of *Waiting for Godot*, the triumph of the rigmarole.

My only serious criticism of Professor Brombert concerns his own use of language. It is depressing to find so good a critic of Flaubert—of all people—scattering academic jargon and archaisms in his prose. The effect is pretentious and may, one hopes, be simply the result of thinking in French and writing in English; but it does match the present academic habit of turning literary criticism into technology. One really cannot write of Flaubert's 'dilection for monstrous forms' or of 'vertiginous proliferation of forms and gestures'; 'dizzying dilation', or 'volitation'; 'lupanar'—when all one means is 'pertaining to a brothel'. Philosophers, psychologists and scientists may, I understand, write of 'fragmentations' that suggest 'a somnambulist and oneiric state'. But who uses the pretentious 'obnuvilate' when they mean 'dim' or 'darkened by cloud'? Imaginative writers know better than to put on this kind of learned dog. The duty of the critic is to literature, not to its surrogates. And if I were performing a textual criticism of this critic I would be tempted to build a whole theory on his compulsive repetition of the word 'velleities'. Words and phrases like these come from the ingenuous and fervent pens of *Bouvard and Pécuchet*.

Literary criticism does not add to its status by opening an intellectual hardware store.

STENDHAL

An Early Outsider

STENDHAL WAS ONE of those gamblers for whom the wheel
of Fortune turned too late. Ignored by almost everyone except
Mérimée and Balzac who considered that *La Chartreuse de
Parme* was the most important French novel of their time, he
declared, without a trace of self-pity, indeed confident in his
blistering vanity, that the wheel would turn 100 years after his
death. In fact in forty years the great egotist was justified by
Zola. For Zola he was: 'a man composed of soul alone. . . . One
always feels him there, coldly attentive to the working of his
machine. Each of his characters is a psychologist's experiment
which he ventures to try on man.' By the beginning of this
century Henri Beyle—the figure hidden secretively behind
more than 200 pseudonyms who had passed his life as a doubt-
fully combatant Napoleonic soldier in Italy and Russia, as a
travelling and loitering journalist and plagiarizing high-class
hack, as a dilettante, petty Consul, ugly and coarse in drawing
rooms, as a misfiring, theorizing lover and a novelist poor in invention who left his great novels abruptly unfinished—had
become a cosmopolitan cult.

One important reason for this is that he knew the lasting
force of that clear, plain, dry and caustic prose style: and knew
that something curt and preposterous in one's style as a person
will have its hour. At certain periods of crises in history and
manners an intelligent man is forced to see that a change of style
is being born. As a youth growing up in the French Revolution
and with youth's need of a persona, he found himself divided
between the eighteenth century idea of 'the man of the world'

and the first intimations of Romantic energy. One had to construct a new self. As an aspiring writer he was drawn to the art of his time: stage comedy—but he soon saw that this had become impossible. Stage comedy depended on a stable class system, fixed social values: these had gone with the Revolution and the post-Napoleonic world. He also saw that the novel was the new form to which the audience would respond but that it would impose a crude, impersonal omniscience and would be about 'other people' grouped in their acceptable categories: the novelist is drowned and effaced in other people, whereas he, Stendhal, secretive, addicted to masks and self-defence, was obsessed by his own intelligent private life, his need to begin constructing a Machiavellian and impervious self from the ground upwards. The egotist lay awake at night, tortured by the question: 'Who am I?' Even more important: 'What shall I make of myself? What is my role? What are the correct tactics?' It is easy to understand why he is the precursor of Romanticism in *La Chartreuse de Parme* and why in *Le Rouge et le Noir* Julien Sorel foreshadows the large population of outsiders and the disaffected formed by the revolutions, wars, social crises, prisons and police states that have revived something of the climate and complacencies of the Napoleonic period. In a recent biography Joanna Richardson says that he was 'a provincial born outside the Establishment, enjoying none of the privileges of birth, wealth or education. His sense of inequality and grievance led him bitterly to make amends. He despised authority, he professed to scorn the nobility and yet—like Julien Sorel—he wanted to conquer the nobility. He ridiculed the dignatories of the Tuileries, and yet, with monotonous persistence, he tried to ensure himself a barony . . . all his life he was conscious of status.' Yet, of course, the desire to be either Sorel or Fabrice was a deeply imaginative conspiracy that sailed far beyond social or political considerations. The egotist's pursuit of personal happiness—*la chasse du bonheur*—led him to the Romantic idealization of solitude and reverie, the brief sublime moment.

The biographer of Stendhal is in competition with a per-petual autobiography—Stendhal has no other subject, in his novels, his letters, his exhaustive *Journal*, in the *Souvenirs d'Egotisme* and *La Vie de Henri Brulard*. He saw himself as a con-spiracy. He was given to minute research into the moral history of his attitudes, so the biographer is left chiefly with the problem of deciding where, if ever, the candour ceased to be fantasy or petulance, where calculation in love was coxcombry, and where they were signs of a fatally split nature. There is no doubt that his celebrated hatred of his father and his sensual passion for his mother, who died when he was seven, reiterated the old Oedipus story, but it was political as well. Stendhal despised his father for being a bourgeois lawyer and a supporter of the Bourbons; very early the boy convinced himself that he was a putative aristocrat and yet at the same time a child of the French Revolution. He also despised his father for being a shrewd Dauphinois and a speculator in property, despised him even more for being unsuccessful in this, and resented the loss of a good deal of his inheritance. Stendhal was even jealous of his widowed father's grief, and went on to imagine that, on the mother's side, the family were of Italian origin and that they combined passionate Italian traits with the pride he oddly loved to call *espagnolisme*. Here, rather than in social snobbery, was the root of his aristocratic idea: he felt he belonged to the élite of another age and another country. Yet his truculence covered deep timidity. His temperament was lazy, but he read and worked like a diligent bourgeois. Only those who work, he said, were equipped for the true end of living—the study of the arts and the pursuit of pleasure.

For one who thought himself born into the wrong class, Stendhal was lucky in 'the bastard', 'the Jesuit' (his father) who gave him a decent allowance and sent him to Paris to study. He was lucky also in family friends—the Darus, who took the con-

ceited youth into their house. He refused to go to the École
Polytechnique, and they got him a job in the Ministry of War.
Stendhal thrived on influence. In a few months, at the age of
seventeen, he was commissioned an officer in Napoleon's re-
serve army in Italy. Italy transfigured him. Italy was freedom;
hearing opera for the first time—'the Scala transformed me'. A
lifelong dislike of France—indeed, the pretence that he was not
really French—began. He fell in love with Angela Pietragrua, a
married woman—older than himself—whom he was too timid
to approach; she fulfilled his need for the remote goddess. There
were untouched remote goddesses to follow; there was also
syphilis, caught in the brothels of Milan, which affected his
health for the rest of his life. The only woman he was really
devoted to for many years was one of his sisters, and in his
letters to her a tutorial figure appears and one begins to see that
he is constructing his own system of self-education and behaviour. The outsider is studying and acting out a role, creating a
self from scratch; it is defiant, touching and a good deal absurd.
In his love affairs—he was determined on seduction—the tactics, the search for a style, the analysis of his amorous cam-
paigns have the fidgetiness of artificial comedy; he spent half
his youth putting obstacles in his own way, as Miss Richardson
says. In the pursuit of these passions, he believed in the *coup de
foudre*: when it occurred, he was paralyzed and in tears; if he
was encouraged, he fell into long storms of melancholy; if he
was victorious, boredom arrived sooner or later, generally
sooner. The perpetual cry of this adolescent, whether he is with
Napoleon's army in Germany or Russia, whether he is back in
Italy, is that he is bored to death. He is one of those who exhaust an experience before the experience occurs—the Romantic malady that becomes a pose and second nature. But if he did
not succeed in creating an impenetrable new self and in becoming the superior man of sensibility, he had fitted himself to
become a master of comedy in which scornful epigram and

abrupt observation go off like rifle shots and leave the dry smell of gunpowder. Each sentence of his plain prose is a separate shock.

The later Romantics were too young for the Napoleonic glory, but in his harsh, sardonic way Stendhal had known it on the battlefield, though not as a fighting officer. From Smolensk he wrote in 1812, when he was twenty-nine:

> How man changes! My former thirst for seeing things is completely quenched, after seeing Milan and Italy, everything repels me by its coarseness. . . . In this ocean of barbarity, there isn't a single sound that replies to my soul.

He was thinking of the music of Cimarosa and his love for Angela Pietragrua. When he watched Moscow burning, he had a toothache and read a few lines of *Virginie*, which revived him morally. He had taken the manuscript of his unfinished *Histoire de la Peinture en Italie* with him, read Mme du Deffand, pillaged a volume of Voltaire, whom he detested, and tried to think of the 'score of comedies' he would write 'between the ages of thirty-four and fifty-four' if only his father would die and leave him some money. He shows off to his correspondents, and rescues an early mistress who had married a Russian (she is very chilly'), but when the great fire starts he seems to keep his head and to display sang-froid—or so people reported. He was unconsciously collecting the material for the superb Waterloo chapter in *La Chartreuse de Parme*, and one catches its accent. (He was not at Waterloo.) Of the beginning of the retreat he wrote in his diary, as one seeing the scene *staged* for his benefit:

> We broke through the lines, arguing with some of the King of Naples' carters. I later noticed that we were following the Tverskoï, or Tver Street. We left the city, illuminated by the finest fire in the world, which formed an immense pyramid which, like the prayers of the faithful, had its base on earth and

its apex in heaven. [Very much like Stendhal's own nature.] The moon appeared above this atmosphere of flame and smoke. It was an imposing sight, but it would have been necessary to be alone or else surrounded by intelligent people in order to enjoy it. What has spoiled the Russian campaign for me is to have taken part in it with people who would have belittled the Colosseum or the Bay of Naples.

An aesthete's comment? Not entirely. It is an introspection we shall see transmuted when we find him examining the illusion of Napoleonic glory. Even before the grand scene the Stendhalian hero is a psychologist. History dished this outsider. He was the victim, he said, of the mediocrity that characterizes an age of transition.

There have been two revivals of interest in Stendhal in this century. In the twenties it was led by Francophiles who used it as a modish attack on the nineteenth century for its denigration of the eighteenth. Stendhal was useful, too, as a distant founder of the parricides' club which thrived after the 1914 war.

The hardness of his ego and his impudence were our admirations; and the 'enclosing reverie' no more than a charming Romantic nostalgia. Stendhal's curt, disabused and iconoclastic manner made the reader of Gide and Proust feel at home. But this movement fizzled out, though it persisted among Beylistes who had a delightful time taping Stendhal's mystifications, footnotes, vanishing tricks, love affairs and changes of address. In the thirties left-wingers and Catholics were frosty about Stendhal's politics and withering about his atheism: he gleamed like an arid Sahara. When the wheel turned, in a second revival, we could feel ourselves to be in something like a Stendhalian situation. Existentialists found the self-inventing man sympathetic; practitioners of *le nouveau roman* looked to the novel without a centre.

In his *Stendhal: Notes on a Novelist*, Mr Robert Adams says:

Perhaps the most enchanting yet terrifying thing about the heroes of Stendhal is the sense that they define their own beings only provisionally and temporarily, in conflicts of thought and action, in negations; without enemies, they are almost without natures and wither away, like Fabrizie, when deprived of danger. I think it is this vision of human nature which allies the novels of Stendhal with the great hollow, reverberant structures of Joyce, and the legerdemain card-houses of Gide; the fact that all systems of thought and feeling are tangential to the nature of their heroes is linked to the circumstances that their central natures are themselves a dark and hollow mystery. From this aspect there is no core or centre to the Stendhal fiction, as there is none to the fiction of Joyce: the more little anagrams and puzzles of correspondence one solves, the less one finds actually being asserted. What the novel means is its shape, its surface, its structure; the arcana of society, like those of thought, are simply emptiness which returns to the surface of life and the solitude of the cynical individual.

Another critic, Victor Brombert, writes in *Stendhal: Fiction and the Themes of Freedom*, that the self-inventing man is a life-long pursuer of freedom:

Neither is it by coincidence that the greatest ecstasies of life take place behind austere and quasi-monastic walls. Ultimately it is freedom from all worldly ambitions, an almost spiritual elation, that Julien Sorel and Fabrice del Donga achieve. . . . Freedom remains a prisoner's dream, and man's vocation is solitude.

This conclusion certainly fits with Stendhal's view that our greatest happiness is in reverie. But it is important here to recall what he wrote about the purpose of *Lucien Leuwen*: it was to be 'exact chemistry: I describe with exactitude what others indicate with a vague and eloquent phrase'. The poetry is to be in the chemistry. Love is a consciously produced effervescence; it produces its transcendant, chemical moment of '*bonheur*'; then the beautiful experiment vanishes. One returns to contemplation until the next 'moment'. And it strikes one, especially when he abruptly creates his unbelievable and preposterous scenes—in this novel the affair of a faked childbirth before witnesses—that his model for the novel was opera, the failure to invent the plausible, or perhaps a success in rising above it.

Yet a political novel like *Lucien Leuwen* is saturated in the social material it offers. It is rich in people who have been 'placed' as astutely as any in Balzac, but with more militancy. The unpopular garrison at Nancy is superbly done, for the minor characters have their own malicious concern for style and role also. They distress the hero. There are portraits of people who are drying up in futile class hatred. Stendhal is as cool—perhaps in his coolness lies the contemporary appeal—about the crude new middle class: he is exact but without the heavy hatred that is sometimes too black and white in Balzac. The following portrait of Mlle Sylvanie, the shopkeeper's daughter, is full yet compressed, poetic yet also ironically of this world. Here the chemistry is indeed exact:

A statue of June, copied from the antique by a modern artist; both subtlety and simplicity are lacking; the lines are massive, but it is a Germanic freshness. Big hands, big feet, very regular features and plenty of coyness, all of which conceals a too obvious pride. And these people are put off by the pride of ladies in good Society! Lucien was particularly struck by her backward tosses of the head, which were full of vulgar nobility, and were evidently meant to recall the dowry of a hundred thousand crowns.

His young women have tenderness and verve: their capacity for growing into their passions is extraordinary. He is always beginning again with his characters for they too are 'making themselves'. And abruptly too. This abruptness is excellent in his portraits of young men; here no novelist in any literature or period has surpassed him, not even Tolstoy. No one has so defined and botanized the fervour, uncertainty, conceit, timidity and single-mindedness of young men, their dash, their shames, their calculation for tactics and gesture. They shed self after self and a date is put to their manners. Stendhal's sense of human beings living now yet transfixed, for an affecting moment, by their future, gives the doctrine of self-invention an ironical perspective which is not often noticeable in its practitioners today.

EÇA DE QUEIROZ

A Portuguese Diplomat

EÇA DE QUEIROZ (1845–1900) is the Portuguese classic of the nineteenth century—not an Iberian Balzac, like Galdos but, rather, a moistened Stendhal, altogether more tender, and, despite his reformist opinions, without theories. He was a diplomat, something of a dandy and gourmet, whose career took him abroad in France, Britain, the Near East, Cuba and the United States, and he was responsive to the intellectual forces that were bringing the European novel to the height of its powers. The temptations of a light and elegant cosmopolitanism must have been strong, for he is above all a novelist of wit and style, and he was amused by the banalities of diplomatic conversation.

But the foreign experience usually serves to strengthen his roots in the Portuguese idiosyncrasy: under the lazy grace, there is the native bluntness and stoicism. A novel like *The Illustrious House of Ramires* is very rich, but it also contrives to be a positive and subtle unraveling of the Portuguese strand in the Iberian temperament. The soft, sensual yet violently alluring Atlantic light glides over his country and his writing, a light more variable and unpredictable than the Castillian; no one could be less 'Spanish' and more western European, yet strong in his native character.

The fear that one is going to be stuck in the quaint, exhaustive pieties of the *folklorico* and regional novel with its tedious local colour, its customs and costumes, soon goes at the sound of his misleadingly simple and sceptical voice. The Portuguese love to pretend to be diminutive in order to surprise by their toughness. Portuguese modesty and nostalgia are national—and devastating. In an introduction to an early short story, 'The Mandarin', he wrote a typically deceptive apology to its French publishers, in which he puts his case. 'Reality, analysis, experimentation or objective certainty,' he said, plague and baffle the Portuguese, who are either lyricists or satirists:

> We dearly love to paint everything blue; a fine sentence will always please me more than an exact notion; the fabled Melusine, who devours human hearts, will always charm our incorrigible imagination more than the very human Marneffe, and we will always consider fantasy and eloquence the only true signs of a superior man. Were we to read Stendhal in Portuguese, we should never be able to enjoy him; what is considered exactitude with him, we should consider sterility. Exact ideas, expressed soberly and in proper form, hardly interest us at all; what charms us is excessive emotion expressed with unabashed plasticity of language.

Eça de Queiroz, we can be certain, did not commit the folly of reading Stendhal in Portuguese. The most exact of novelists, he read him in French, and the comedy is that he was very much a romantic Stendhalian—he was even a Consul-General—and in exactitude a Naturalist. Under the irony and the grace, there are precision and sudden outbursts of ecstasy and of flamboyant pride in a prose that coils along and then suddenly vibrates furiously when emotion breaks through, or breaks into unashamed burlesque.

He was an incessant polisher of his style. The following passage, from *The City and the Mountains*, shows his extraordinary power of letting rip and yet keeping his militant sense of comedy in command. His hero has just been thrown over by a cocotte in Paris. His first reaction is to go and eat an expensive meal of lobster and duck washed down by champagne and Burgundy; the second is to rush back to the girl's house, punching the cushions of the cab as he goes, for in the cushions he sees, in his fury, 'the huge bush of yellow hair in which my soul was lost one evening, fluttered and struggled for two months, and soiled itself for ever'. He fights the driver and the servants at the house, and then he goes off home, drunk and maddened:

Stretched out on the ancestral bed of Dom 'Galleon', with my boots on my pillow and my hat over my eyes, I laughed a sad laugh at this burlesque world. . . . Suddenly I felt a horrible anguish. It was She. It was Madame Colombe who appeared out of the flame of the candle, jumped on my bed, undid my waistcoat, sunk herself onto my breast, put her mouth to my heart, and began to suck my blood from it in long slow gulps. Certain of death now, I began to scream for my Aunt Vicencia; I hung from the bed to try to sink into my sepulchre which I dimly discerned beneath me on the carpet, through the final fog of death—a little round sepulchre, glazed and made of porcelain, with a handle. And over my own sepulchre, which so irreverently chose to resemble a chamberpot, I vomited the lobster, the duck, the pimientos and the Burgundy. Then after a super-human effort, with the roar of a lion, feeling that not only my innards but my very soul were emptying themselves in the process, I vomited up Madame Colombe herself. . . . I put my hat back over my eyes so as not to feel the rays of the sun. It was a new Sun, a spiritual Sun which was rising over my life. I slept like a child softly rocked in a cradle of wicker by my Guardian Angel.

This particular novel savages Paris as the height of city civilization, a wealthy Utopia; it argues for the return to nature in the Portuguese valleys. Eça de Queiroz can still astonish us in this satire with his catalogue of mechanical conveniences. They are remarkably topical. (His theatre-telephone, for example, is our television or radio.) The idea of a machine civilization that has drained off the value of human life recalls Forster's *The Machine Stops*. Maliciously Queiroz describes our childish delight in being ravished by a culture of affluence or surfeit. He was in at the birth of boredom and conspicuous waste. One brilliant fantasy of the hero is that he is living in a city where the men and women are simply made of newspaper, where the houses are made of books and pamphlets and the streets paved with them. Change printed-matter to the McLuhanite Muzak culture of today, and the satire is contemporary. The hero returns to the droll, bucolic kindness of life in Portugal, in chapters that have the absurd beauty of, say, Oblomov's dream.

The prose carries this novel along, but one has to admit there is a slightly faded *fin de siècle* air about it. *The Illustrious House of Ramires* is a much better rooted and more ambitious work. Obviously his suggestion that the Portuguese are not experimentalists is a Portuguese joke, for the book is a novel within a novel, a comedy of the relation of the unconscious with quotidian experience. One is tricked at first into thinking one is caught up in a rhetorical tale of chivalry *à la* Walter Scott; then one changes one's mind and treats its high-flown historical side as one of those Romances that addled the mind of Don Quixote; finally one recognizes this element as an important part of psychological insight. What looks like old hat reveals its originality.

Ramires is an ineffectual and almost ruined aristocrat who is rewriting the history of his Visigothic ancestors in order to raise his own morale. It is an act of personal and political therapy. He is all for liberal reform, but joins the party of Regenerators or traditionalists whose idea is to bring back the days of Portugal's greatness. Ramires revels in the battles, sieges and slaughterings of his famous family and—while he is writing this vivid and bloody stuff—he is taking his mind off the humiliations of his own life. The heir of the Ramires is a dreamer. He is a muddler and his word is never to be relied on. He shuffles until finally he gets himself in the wrong. This is because he is timid and without self-confidence: he deceives a decent peasant over a contract and then, losing his self-control when the peasant protests, has him sent to prison on the pretext that the man tried to assault him. Then rage abates and he hurriedly gets the man out of prison.

Ramires has a long feud with a local philandering politician of the opposite party, because this man has jilted his sister; yet, he makes it up with the politician in order to get elected as a deputy—only to see that the politician does this only to be sure of seducing the sister. The price of political triumph is his sister's honour and happiness. How can he live with himself after that? Trapped continually by his pusillanimity, he tries to recover by writing one more chapter of his novel of chivalry, fleeing to an ideal picture of himself. What saves him—and this is typical of the irony of Queiroz—is his liability to insensate physical rage, always misplaced. He half kills a couple of ruffians on the road by horsewhipping them and, incidentally, gives a fantastically exaggerated account of the incident; but the event and the lie give him self-confidence. He is a hero at last! He begins to behave with a comic mixture of cunning and dignity. He saves his sister, becomes famous as a novelist, long-headedly makes a rich marriage, and tells the King of Portugal that he is an upstart. Total triumph of luck, accident, pride, impulse in a helplessly devious but erratically generous character loved by everyone. Tortured by uncertainty, carried away by idealism and feeling, a curious mixture of the heroic and the shady, he has become welded into a man.

And who is this man? He is not simply Ramires, the aristocrat. He is—Portugal itself: practical, stoical, shifty, its pride in its great past, its pride in pride itself raging inside like an unquenchable sadness There is iron in the cosiness of Queiroz. He has the disguised militancy of the important comedians. His comic scenes are very fine, for there is always a serious or symbolical body to them. His sensuality is frank. His immense detail in the evocation of Portuguese life is always on the move;

and the mixture of disingenuousness and genuine feeling in all his characters makes every incident piquant.

A match-making scene takes place in the boring yet macabre crypt where the ancestors of Ramires are buried. Ramires knows his ancestors would have killed his sister's lover; all *he* can do is to pray feverishly that her silly, jolly, cuckolded husband will never find out. Prudence and self-interest suggest caution; not mere caution but an anxious mixture of politeness, kindness, worldly-wisdom and a stern belief in dignity, if you can manage it, plus the reflection that even the most inexcusable adulteries may have a sad, precious core of feeling. Ramires is not a cynic; nor is Eça de Queiroz. He is saved from that by his lyrical love of life, his abandonment—for the moment—to the unpredictable sides of his nature; in other words, by his candour and innocence. His people live by their imagination from minute to minute. They are constantly impressionable; yet they never lose their grasp of the practical demands of their lives—the interests of land, money, illness, politics.

In the historical pages of Ramires's historical novel, there is a double note, romantic yet sardonic. The scenes are barbarous and bloody—they express the unconscious of Ramires, the dreams that obsess him and his nation—but the incidental commentary is as dry as anything in Stendhal. During a siege:

> The bailiff waddled down the blackened, spiral stairway to the steps outside the keep. Two liegemen, their lances at their shoulders, returning from a round, were talking to the armourer who was painting the handles of new javelins yellow and scarlet and lining them up against the wall to dry.

Yet a few lines farther down, we shall see a father choose to see his son murdered, rather than surrender his honour. The violence of history bursts out in Ramires's own life in the horse-whipping scene I have mentioned earlier. The sensation—he finds—is sublime. But when Ramires gets home his surprise at the sight of real blood on his whip and clothes shatters him. He does not want to be as murderous as the knights of old. He is all for humanity and charity. He was simply trying to solve his psychological difficulty: that he had never, in anything until then, imposed his own will, but had yielded to the will of others who were simply corrupting him and leaving him to wake up to one more humiliation. It is a very contemporary theme.

The making of this novel and indeed all the others, is the restless mingling of poetry, sharp realism and wit. Queiroz is untouched by the drastic hatred of life that underlies Naturalism: he is sad rather than indignant that every human being is compromised; indeed this enables him to present his characters from several points of view and to explore the unexpectedness of human nature. The elements of self-surprise and self-imagination are strong; and his excellent prose glides through real experience and private dream in a manner that is leading on toward the achievements of Proust. His translators have done their difficult task pretty well: Roy Campbell being outstanding.

GALDOS

A Spanish Balzac

PEREZ GALDOS IS the supreme Spanish novelist of the 19th century. His scores of novels are rightly compared with the work of Balzac and Dickens who were his masters, and even with Tolstoy's. Why then has he been almost totally neglected by foreigners? One reason is that wherever Spanish city life had anything in common with Western European societies, it appeared to be out of date and a provincial parody; and where there was no resemblance it was interpreted by foreign collectors of the outlandish and picturesque. One of the anglicized characters in his longest novel *Fortunata and Jacinta* returns to England saying, bitterly, that all the British want from Spain is tourist junk—and this in 1873! One could read the great Russians without needing to go to Russia; their voice carried across the frontiers. To grasp Galdos—it was felt—one had to go to Spain and submit to Spanish formality, pride and claustrophobia. Few readers outside of academic life did so.

These objections no longer have the same force and it is more likely that the great achievement of Galdos can be recognized here today. A few years ago, his short novel *The Spendthrifts* (*La de Bringas*) was translated by Gerald Brenan and Gamel Woolsey and now we have Lester Clark's complete translation of the 1,100 pages of his most ambitious novel. It takes its place among those Victorian masterpieces that have presented the full-length portrait of a city.

The originality of Galdos springs, in part, from the fact that he was a silent outsider—he was brought up in the Canaries

under English influences. In time he learned how to drift to
the Spanish pace and then, following Balzacian prescription
and energy, set out to become 'the secretary of history'. He
is reported to have been a quiet and self-effacing man and this
novel gets its inspiration from the years he spent listening to
the voices of Madrid. His intimacy with every social group is
never the sociologist's; it is the personal intimacy of the artist,
indeed it can be said he disappears as a person and *becomes* the
people, streets and kitchens, cafés and churches. This total
absorption has been held against him: the greatest novelists,
in some way, impose—the inquirer does not. Yet this very
passivity matches a quality in Spanish life; and anyway he is
not the dry inquirer; his inquiry is directed by feeling and
especially by tolerant worship of every motion of the heart, a
tenderness for its contradictions and its dreams, for its everyday
impulses and also for those that are vibrant, extreme—even
insane. He is an excellent story-teller, he loves the inventiveness
of life itself. Preaching nothing overtly, he is a delicate and
patient psychologist. It is extraordinary to find a novel written
in the 1880s that documents the changes in the cloth trade, the
rise and fall of certain kinds of café, the habits of usurers,
politicians and catholic charities but also probes the fantasies
and dreams of the characters and follows their inner thoughts.
Galdos is fascinated by the psychology of imitation and the
primitive unconscious. He changes the 'point of view' without
regard to the rules of the novelist's game. We are as sure of
the likeness of each character as we are of the figures in a
Dutch painting and yet they are never set or frozen, they are
always moving in space in the Tolstoyan fashion. The secret
of the gift of Galdos lies, I think, in his timing, his leisurely
precision and above all in his ear for dialogue; his people live
in speech, either to themselves or to each other. He was a born
assimilator of speech of all kinds from the rich skirling dialect
of the slums or the baby-language of lovers, to the even more

difficult speech of people who are trying to express or evade more complex thoughts.

The dramatic thread that runs through the panorama of life in Madrid in 1873 is the story of the love and destructive jealousy of two women. Fortunata is a beautiful and ignorant slum girl who is seduced by the idle son of rich shopkeepers before his marriage and bears him a son who dies. Jacinta becomes the young man's beautiful but pathetic wife, tormented less by her husband's love affairs than by the fact that she cannot bear children. The deserted Fortunata takes up a life of promiscuity from which a feeble and idealistic young chemist sets about rescuing her. She longs to be a respectable wife and is bullied into going into a convent for a time so that she can be reformed. But she cannot get over her love of her seducer and although she comes out of the convent and marries the chemist, she feels no affection for him. He is indeed impotent, and going from one philosophical or religious mania to another, ends by becoming insane and murderous in his jealousy of her first lover who has resumed the pursuit. It becomes a battle, therefore, between the bourgeois wife and the loose woman. Fortunata is a tragic figure of the people, a victim of her own sensual impulses who, in the end, has a second child by her seducer and regards herself as his true respectable wife because the other is barren. But her child is taken over by the rich and legitimate wife and Fortunata dies raging. The scene is overwhelming. The last time I wept over a novel was in reading *Tess* when I was 18. Fifty years later Fortunata has made me weep again. Not simply because of her death but because Galdos had portrayed a woman whole in all her moods. In our own 19th-century novels this situation would be melodramatic and morally overweighted—see George Eliot's treatment of Hetty Sorrel—but in Galdos there is no such excess. The bourgeois wife is in her limited way as attractive as Fortunata.

Among the large number of Fortunata's friends, enemies and neighbours, there are two or three portraits that are in their own way as powerful as hers. First there is Mauricia la Dura, an incorrigible, violent and drunken prostitute to whom Fortunata is drawn against her will in the convent. Mauricia attracts by the terror and melancholy of her face. She is a genuine Spanish primitive. There is a long and superb scene in which she manages to get hold of some brandy in the convent and passes from religious ecstasy to blasphemy, theft and violence. It is a mark of the great novelist that he can invent a fantastic scene like this and then, later on, take us into the mind of the violent girl after she has got over her mania. Galdos knows how to return to the norm:

'I was beside myself. I only remember I saw the Blessed Virgin and then I wanted to go into the church to get the Holy Sacrament. I dreamt I ate the Host—I've never had such a bad bout. . . . The things that go through your mind when the devil goes to your head. Believe me because I'm telling you. When I came to my senses I was so ashamed. . . . The only one I hated was that Chaplain. I'd have bitten chunks out of him. But not the nuns. I wanted to beg their forgiveness; but my dignity wouldn't let me. What upset me most was having thrown a bit of brick at Doña Guillermina, I'll never forget that—never —And I'm so afraid that when I see her coming along the street my face colours up and I go by on the other side so that she won't see me.'

Doña Guillermina, a rich woman who has given up everything for the rescue work, is another fine portrait of the practical good-humoured saint, a sort of Santa Teresa who— and this shows the acuteness of the novelist's observation—can be frightened, a shade automatic, and sometimes totally at a loss. Against her must be placed Doña Lupe, a lower-middle-class moneylender. She is a miser who shouts to her maid:

'Clean your feet on the next-door shoe-scraper . . . because the fewer people who use ours, the more we gain.'

But at the wedding of Fortunata to her nephew we recognise Doña Lupe as more than a grotesque. Galdos is superior to Balzac in not confining people to a single dominant passion:

> Once back in the house, Doña Lupe seemed to have burst from her skin for she grew and multiplied remarkably. . . . You would have thought there were three or four widow Jaurequis in the house, all functioning at the same time. Her mind was boiling at the possibility of the lunch not going well. But if it turned out well what a triumph! Her heart beat violently, pumping feverish heat all over her body, and even the ball of cottonwool at her breast [she had had one breast removed] seemed to be endowed with its share of life, being allowed to feel pain and worry.

The final large character is Max, the husband of Fortunata. She dislikes him, but he has 'saved' her. Puny and sexless, Max begins to seek relief in self-aggrandizement, first of all in prim and ingenuous idealism; when he realizes his marriage is null and that his 'cure' of Fortunata is a failure, he turns to experimenting with pills and hopes to find a commerical cure-all. His efforts are incompetent and dangerous. The next stage is paranoia caused by sexual jealousy. He moves on to religious mania: thinks of murder and then invites his wife to join him in a suicide pact, in order to rid the world of sin. For a while he is mad and then, suddenly, he recovers and 'sees his true situation'—but recovery turns him into a blank non-being. Here we see Galdos' belief in imitative neurosis, for in a terrible scene poor Fortunata is infected with her husband's discarded belief in violence. She declares she will love him utterly, if only he will go and murder her libertine lover. But Max has fallen into complete passivity: he enters a monastery where he will become a solitary mystic—and he does not realize that the monastery he has chosen is, in fact, an asylum.

It is surprising to find this Dostoevskian study in Galdos but, of course, Spanish life can offer dozens of such figures. They are examples of what Spanish writers have often noted: the tendency of the self to be obdurately as it is and yet to project itself into some universal extreme, to think of itself mystically as God or the universe. But usually—as Galdos showed in his portrait of the ivory-carving civil servant in *The Spendthrifts*—such characters are simply bizarre and finicking melancholics. Around them stand the crowd of self-dramatizers in the old cafés, the pious church-going ladies, the various types of priest, the shouters of the slums. What is more important is his ability to mount excellent scenes, and in doing so, to follow the feelings of his people with a tolerant and warm detachment. He is never sentimental. There is one fine example of his originality and total dissimilarity from other European novelists in his long account of Jacinta's honeymoon. The happy girl cannot resist acting unwisely: little by little she tries to find out about her husband's early love affair, mainly to increase the excitement of her own love. No harm comes of this dangerous love game, but we realize that here is a novelist who can describe early married life without reserves and hit upon the piquancy that is its spell. I can think of no honeymoon in literature to match this one. The fact is that Galdos accepts human nature without resentment.

MACHADO DE ASSIS

A Brazilian

FEW ENGLISH READERS had heard of Machado de Assis before 1953. His novel *Braz Cubas* was translated in that year by
William Grossman, under the title of *Epitaph for a Small Winner*,
forty-five years after his death. There was also a very good
translation published in 1955, by E. Percy Ellis. Since then we
have been able to read *Dom Casmurro*, a collection of stories
called *The Psychiatrist*, and *Esau and Jacob*, which has awkward
inflections of truck-driver's American in the dialogue. Assis is
spoken of as Brazil's greatest novelist. He was born in 1839 and
his work comes out of the period marked by the fall of the
monarchy, the liberation of the slaves and the establishment of
the Republic. He pre-dates the later European immigration
which was to change the great cities of Brazil completely and
introduce new Mediterranean and Teutonic strains into the
Brazilian character.

Assis said that his simple novels were written 'in the ink of
mirth and melancholy'. The simplicity is limpid and delightful,
but it is a deceptive distillation. One is always doubtful about
how to interpret the symbolism and allegory that underlie his
strange love stories and his impressions of a wealthy society.
The picture of Rio could not be more precise, yet people and
city seem to be both physically there and not there. The actual
life he evokes has gone, but it is reillumined or revived by his
habit of seeing people as souls fluttering like leaves blown away
by time. In this he is very modern: his individuals have the
force of anonymities. His aim, in all his books, seems to be to
rescue a present moment just before it sinks into the past or

reaches into its future. He is a mixture of comedian, lyrical poet, psychological realist and utterly pessimistic philosopher. We abruptly fall into dust and that is the end. But it would be quite wrong to identify him with, the sated bankers, politicians, sentimental roués and bookish diplomats who appear in the novels. His tone is far removed from the bitter-sweet mockery and urbane scepticism of, say, Anatole France; and it is free of that addiction to rhetorical French romanticism which influenced all South American literature during the nineteenth century. He eventually became an Anglophile.

Epitaph for a Small Winner was a conscious break with France. It is a lover's account of an affair with a friend's wife. The affair is broken—perhaps luckily—by circumstance and the writer concludes that there was a small surplus of fortune in his life: 'I had no progeny, I transmitted to no one the legacy of our misery.' To get a closer idea of Assis, one must think chiefly of Sterne, Swift and Stendhal. He is an exact, original, economical writer, who pushes the machinery of plot into the background. His short chapters might be a moralist's notes. Like Sterne, he is obsessed with Time, eccentric, even whimsical; like Stendhal, accurate and yet passionate; like Swift, occasionally savage. But the substance is Brazilian. It is not a matter of background, though there is the pleasure of catching sight of corners of Rio and Petropolis—the little St Germain up in the mountains where Court society used to go to get out of the damp heat. Some of the spirit caught by Assis still survives in Rio: under the gaiety there is something grave; under the corruption something delicate; under the fever something passive and contemplative. The Portuguese *saudade* can be felt within the violence; and a preoccupation with evasive manoeuvre, as it occurs in games or elaborate artificial comedy, is a constant recourse and solace, in every department of life. Like the Portuguese before Salazar, the Brazilians attempted to circumvent their own violence by playing comedies.

Assis' career could be seen as a triumph of miscegenation. He was born in one of the *favelas* or shack slums that are dumped on the hills in the very centre of Rio, the son of a mulatto house-painter and a Portuguese woman. She died and he had no education beyond what he picked up in an aristocratic house where his stepmother worked as a cook. He learned French from the local baker, got a job as a typesetter and eventually turned journalist. It is not surprising that he was sickly, epileptic and industrious and that one of his interests was insanity. Like many other Latin American writers, he supported himself by working in the civil service; but in his spare time he wrote thirty miscellaneous volumes and became President of the Brazilian Academy.

It is said that he is even more admired in Brazil for his short stories than for his novels and from the small selection called *The Psychiatrist*, one can see why : here the dreamy monotone of his novels vanishes. From story to story the mood changes. He astonishes by passing from satire to artifice, from wit to the emotional weight of a tale like 'Midnight Mass' or to the terrible realism of 'Admiral's Night,' a story of slave-hunting which could have come out of Flaubert. In a way, all the novels, of Assis are constructed by a short-story-teller's mind, for he is a vertical, condensing writer who slices through the upholstery of the realist novel into what is essential. He is a collector of the essences of whole lives and does not labour with chronology, jumping back or forward confidently in time as it pleases him. A man will be described simply as handsome or coarse, a woman as beautiful or plain; but he will plunge his hand into them and pull out the vitalizing paradox of their inner lives, showing how they are themselves and the opposite of themselves and how they are in flux.

In *Esau and Jacob* there is a fine comic portrait of the pushing wife of a wobbly politician who has just lost his governorship. She is a woman who kisses her friends 'as if she wanted to eat them alive, to consume them, not with hate, to put them inside her, deep inside'. She revels in power and—a quality Assis admires in his women—is innocent of moral sense:

> It was so good to arrive in the province, all announced, the visits aboard ship, the landing, the investitures, the officials' greetings. . . . Even the vilification by the opposition was agreeable. To hear her husband called tyrant, when she knew he had a pigeon's heart, did her soul good. The thirst for blood that they attributed to him, when he did not even drink wine, the mailed fist of a man that was a kid glove, his immorality, barefaced effrontery, lack of honour, all the unjust strong names, she loved to read as if they were eternal truths—where were they now?

The grotesque, Assis says in one of his epigrams, is simply ferocity in disguise: but here the beauty of the grotesque comes from tolerance. Sometimes people are absurd, sometimes wicked, sometimes good. Timidity may lead to virtue, deception to love; our virtues are married to our vices. The politician's wife gets to work on her husband and skilfully persuades him to change parties. He is morally ruined but this stimulates his self-esteem. The pair simply become absurd. This particular chapter of comedy is very Stendhalian—say, from *Lucien Leuwen*.

Esau and Jacob is, on the face of it, a political allegory, observed by an old diplomat. He has been the unsuccessful lover of Natividade, the wife of a rich banker, a lady given to a rather sadistic fidelity and to exaltation. She gives birth to identical twin boys and consults an old sorceress about their destiny. She is told they will become great men and will perpetually quarrel. And so they do. As they rise to greatness, one becomes a monarchist and defender of the old stable traditions, the other a republican and a believer in change and the future. They fall in love with the same girl, Flora, who can scarcely tell them apart and who, fatally unable to make up her mind about them, fades away and dies. (People die as inconsequently as they do in E. M. Forster.) The meaning of the allegory may be that Natividade is the old Brazil and that Flora is the girl of the new Brazil who cannot decide between the parties. But underlying this is another allegory. One young man looks to the Past, the other to the Future; the girl is the Present, puzzled by its own breathless evanescence, and doomed. All the people in Assis seem to be dissolving in time, directed by their Destiny—the old sorceress up in the *favela*.

The theme of *Esau and Jacob* is made for high-sounding dramatic treatment; but Assis disposes of that by his cool, almost disparaging tenderness as he watches reality and illusion change places. In *Dom Casmurro* we have another of his cheated lovers. A young seminarist has been vowed to the Church by his mother, but is released from his vow by a sophistry, so that he can marry a girl whom he adores and who patiently intrigues to get him. Their love affair and marriage are exquisitely described. But the shadow of the original sophistry is long. Dom Casmurro had made a friend at the seminary, and this friend becomes the father of the boy Dom Casmurro thinks his own. When the boy grows up, Dom Casmurro finds that he is haunted by this copy of his friend. All die, for the subject is illusion. The concern with exchanged identities and doubles— very much a theme of the Romantic movement—is not left on the level of irony or paradox: Assis follows it into our moral nature, into the double quality of our sensibility, and the uncertainty of what we are. We are the sport of nature, items in a game.

One sees how much Assis has in common with his contemporary, Pirandello. With the growth of agnosticism at the end of the nineteenth century, people played intellectually with the occult—one of the Assis bankers consults a spiritualist—and amused themselves with conundrums about illusion and reality, sanity and insanity. In *The Psychiatrist* a doctor puts the whole town into his asylum. But there is something heartless and brittle in Pirandello. The Brazilian is warmer, gentler. One does not feel about him, as about Pirandello, that intellect and feeling are separate. At his most airily speculative and oblique, Assis still contrives to give us the sense of a whole person, all of a love affair, a marriage, an illness, a career and a society, by looking at their fragments. There is a curious moment in the *Epitaph for a Small Winner* when we are told that the poor, wronged, unhappy woman who is used by the clandestine lovers as a screen for their affair was perhaps born to have just that role and use in their lives: the reflection is good, for if it conveys the egoism of the lovers, it also conveys the sense of unconscious participation which is the chief intuition of Assis as an artist, and which makes his creatures momentarily solid.

The Myth Makers

IT HAS OFTEN been said of the Spanish nature and—by extension—of those who have inherited Iberian influences in South America, that the ego is apt to leap across middle ground and see itself as a universe. The leap is to an All. The generalization itself skips a great deal too, but it is a help towards beginning to understand the astonishing richness of the South American novelists of recent years. Their 'All'—and I think of Vargas Llosa and Garcia Márquez among others—is fundamentally 'the people', not in the clichés of political rhetoric but in the sense of millions of separate lives, no longer anonymous but physically visible, awash in historical memory and with identities.

After reading *Leaf Storm*, the novella written by Gabriel Garcia Márquez when he was only nineteen, but not published until 1955, one sees what a distance lies between this effort and his masterpiece *One Hundred Years of Solitude*. The young author sows the seed of a concern with memory, myth and the nature of time which bursts into lovely shameless blossom in his later book. We get our first glimpse of the forgotten town of Macondo (obviously near Cartagena), a primitive place, once a naïve colonial Eden; then blasted by the 'leaf storm' of the invading foreign banana-companies, and finally a ghost town, its founders forgotten. Shut up in a room in one of its remaining family houses is an unpleasant doctor who 'lives on grass'—a vegetarian?—whom the town hates because he once refused to treat some men wounded after a civil rising. Now, secluded for goodness knows how many years, he has hanged himself, and the question is whether the town will riot and refuse to have him buried. The thing to notice is that, like so many South American novelists, Márquez was even then drawn to the inordinate character—not necessarily a giant or saga-like hero, but someone who has exercised a right to extreme conduct or aberration. Such people fulfil a new country's need for legends. A human being is required to be a myth, his spiritual value lies in the inflating of his tale.

Far better than *Leaf Storm* are some of the short stories in the new collection, and one above all. 'The Handsomest Drowned Man in the World'. The story is an exemplary guide to the art of Márquez, for it is a celebration of the myth-making process. Somewhere on the seashore children are found playing with the body of a drowned man, burying it, digging it up again, burying it. Fishermen take the corpse to the village, and while the men go off to inquire about missing people, the women are left to prepare the body for burial. They scrape off the crust of little shells and stones and weed and mess and coral in which the body is wrapped and then they see the man within:

> They noticed that he bore his death with pride for he did not have the lonely look of other drowned men who came out of the sea or that haggard needy look of men who drowned in rivers . . . he was the tallest, strongest, most virile and best built man they had ever seen . . . They thought if that magnificent man had lived in the village, his house would have had the widest doors, the highest ceiling, and the strongest floor, his bedstead would have been made from a midship frame held together by iron bolts and his wife would have been the happiest woman. They thought he would have had so much authority he could have drawn fish out of the sea simply by calling their names.

The women imagine him in their houses; they see that because he is tall, the doors and ceilings of their houses would have to be higher and they tell him affectionately to 'mind his head' and so on. The dead god has liberated so much fondness and wishing that when the body is at last formally buried at sea it is not weighed down by an anchor, for the women and the men too hope that the dead man will realize that he is welcome to come back at any time.

There is nothing arch or whimsical in the writing of this fable. The prose of Márquez is plain, exact, subtle and springy and easily leaps into the comical and the exuberant, as we find in *One Hundred Years of Solitude*. In that book the history of the Buendía families and their women in three or four generations is written as a hearsay report on the growth of the little Colombian town; it comes to life because it is continuously leaping out of fact into the mythical and the myth is comic. One obvious analogy is with Rabelais. It is suggested, for example, that Aureliano Segundo's sexual orgies with his concubine are so enjoyable that his own livestock catch the fever. Animals and birds are unable to stand by and do nothing. The rancher's life is a grandiose scandal; the 'bonecrusher' in bed is a heroic glutton who attracts 'fabulous eaters' from all over the country. There is an eating duel with a lady known as 'The Elephant'. The duel lasted from a Saturday to a Tuesday, but it had its elegance:

> While Aureliano ate with great bites, overcome by the anxiety of victory, The Elephant was slicing her meat with the art of a surgeon and eating it unhurriedly and even with a certain pleasure. She was gigantic and sturdy, but over her colossal form a tenderness of femininity prevailed . . . later on when he saw her consume a side of veal without breaking a single rule of good table manners, he commented that this most delicate, fascinating and insatiable proboscidian was in a certain way the ideal woman.

The duel is beautifully described and with a dozen inventive touches, for once Márquez gets going there is no controlling his fancy. But note the sign of the master: the story is always brought back to ordinary experience in the end. Aureliano was ready to eat to the death and indeed passes out. The scene has taken place at his concubine's house. He gasps out a request to be taken to his wife's house because he had promised not to die in his concubine's bed; and she, who knows how to behave, goes and shines up his patent leather boots that he had always planned to wear in his coffin. Fortunately he survives. It is very important to this often ruthless, licentious and primitive epic that there is a deep concern for propriety and manners.

As a fable or phantasmagoria *One Hundred Years of Solitude* succeeds because of its comic animality and its huge exaggerations which somehow are never gross and indeed add a certain delicacy. Márquez seems to be sailing down the blood stream of his people as they innocently build their town in the swamp, lose it in civil wars, go mad in the wild days of the American banana company and finally end up abandoned. The story is a social history but not as it is found in books but as it muddles its way forward or backward among the sins of family life and the accidents of trade. For example, one of the many Aurelianos has had the luck and intelligence to introduce ice to Macondo. To extend the ice business was impossible without getting the railroad in. This is how Márquez introduces the railroad:

> Aureliano Centeno, overwhelmed by the abundance of the factory, had already begun to experiment in the production of ice with a base of fruit juices instead of water, and without knowing it or thinking about it, he conceived the essential fundamentals for the invention of sherbet. In that way he planned to diversify the production of an enterprise he considered his own, because his brother showed no signs of returning after the rains had passed and the whole summer had gone by with no news of him. At the start of another winter a woman who was washing clothes in the river during the hottest time of the day ran screaming down the main street in an alarming state of commotion.

'It's coming,' she finally explained. 'Something frightful like a kitchen dragging a village behind it.'

There are scores of rippling pages that catch the slippery comedies and tragedies of daily life, at the speed of life itself: the more entangled the subject the faster the pace. Márquez is always ready to jump to extremes; it is not enough for a girl to invite two school friends to her family's house, she invites seventy horrible girls and the town has to be ransacked for seventy chamber pots. Crude or delicate an incident may be, but it is singular in the way ordinary things are. Almost every sentence is a surprise and the surprise is, in general, really an extension of our knowledge or feeling about life, and not simply a trick. Ursula, the grandmother of the Buendía tribe, the one stable character, is a repository of superstitious wisdom, i.e., superstition, is a disguised psychological insight. In her old age, we see her revising her opinions, especially one about babies who 'weep in the womb'. She discusses this with her husband and he treats the idea as a joke. He says such children will become ventriloquists; she thinks that they will be prophets. But now, surveying the harsh career of her son who has grown up to be a proud and heartless fighter of civil wars, she says that 'only the unloving' weep in the womb. And those who cannot love are in need of more compassion than others. An insight? Yes, but also it brings back dozens of those talks one has had in Spain (and indeed in South America) where people kill the night by pursuing the bizarre or the extreme by-ways of human motive.

In no derogatory sense, one can regard this rapid manner of talk—non-stop, dry and yet fantastical—as characteristic of café culture: lives pouring away in long bouts of chatter. In North America its characteristic form is the droll monologue; in South America the fantasy is—in my limited reading—more agile and imaginative, richer in laughter and, of course, especially happy in its love of the outrageous antics of sexual life.

One Hundred Years of Solitude denies interpretation. One could say that a little Arcady was created but was ruined by the 'Promethian ideas' that came into the head of its daring founder. Or that little lost towns have their moment—as civilizations do —and are then obliterated. Perhaps the moral is, as Márquez says, that 'races condemned to one hundred years of solitude do not get a second chance on earth'. The notion of 'the wind passeth over it and it is gone' is rubbed in; so also is the notion Borges has used, of a hundred years or even infinite time being totally discernible in a single minute. But what Márquez retrieves from the history he has surveyed is an Homeric laughter.

Life is ephemeral but dignified by fatality: the word 'ephemeral' often crops up in *The Autumn of the Patriarch*, which has been well translated by Gregory Rabassa—the original would be beyond even those foreigners who read Spanish.

The Patriarch who gives the novel its moral theme is the elusive despot of a South American republic and we hear him in the scattered voices of his people and his own. As a young wild bull he is the traditional barefoot peasant leader; later he is the confident monster ruthlessly collecting the spoils of power, indifferent to murder and massacre, sustained by his simple peasant mother, surviving by cunning. Still later, in old age, he is a puppet manipulated by the succeeding juntas, who are selling off the country to exploiters, a Caliban cornered but tragic, with a terrifying primitive will to survive. His unnamed republic looks out on the Caribbean from a barren coast from which the sea has receded, so that he believes, as superstitiously as his people do, that foreigners have even stolen the sea.

By the time the novel opens he is a myth to his people. Those who think they have seen him have probably seen only his double, though they may have glimpsed his hand waving from a limousine. He himself lives among the remnants of his concubines and the lepers and beggars that infest the Presidential fort. His mother is dead. He stamps round on his huge feet and is mainly concerned with milking his cows in the dairy attached to his mansion. Power is in the hands of an untrusted Minister. The President no longer leaves the place but drowses as he reads of speeches he has never made, celebrations he has never attended, applause he has never heard, in the newspaper of which only one copy is printed and solely for himself. He is, in short, an untruth; a myth in the public mind, a dangerous animal decaying in 'the solitary vice' of despotic power, fearing one more attempt at assassination and, above all, the ultimate solitude of death.

At first sight the book is a capricious mosaic of multiple narrators. We slide from voice to voice in the narrative without warning, in the course of the long streaming sentences of consciousness. But the visual, animal realism is violent and forever changing: we are swept from still moments of domestic fact to vivid fantasy, back and forth in time from, say, the arrival of the first Dutch discoverers to the old man looking at television, in the drift of hearsay and memory.

The few settled characters are like unforgettable news flashes that disturb and disappear: the richness of the novel will not be grasped in a single reading. We can complain that it does not progress but returns upon itself in widening circles. The complaint is pointless: the spell lies in the immediate force of its language and the density of narrative. We can be lost in those interminable sentences and yet once one has got the hang of the transitions from one person to the next it is all as sharp as the passing moment is because Márquez is the master weaver of the real and the conjectured. His descriptive power astounds at once, in the first forty pages where the narrator is a naïve undefined 'we', i.e., the people. They break into the fortress of the tragic monster and find their Caliban dead among the cows that have long ago broken out of the dairy and graze off the carpets in the salons of the ruined Presidencia and even have appeared, lowing like speakers, on the balconies. This is from the opening scene:

> When the first vultures began to arrive, rising up from where they had dozed on the cornices of the charity hospital, they came from farther inland, they came in successive waves, out of the horizon of the sea of dust where the sea had been, for a whole day they flew in slow circles of the house of power until a king with bridal feathers and a crimson ruff gave a silent order and that breaking of glass began, that breeze of a great man dead, that in and out of vultures through the windows imaginable only in a house which lacked authority, so we dared go in too and in the deserted sanctuary we found the rubble of grandeur, the body that had been pecked at, the smooth maiden hands with the ring of power on the bone of the third finger, and his whole body was sprouting tiny lichens and parasitic animals from the depths of the sea, especially in the armpits and the groin, and he had the canvas truss of his herniated testicle which was the only thing that had escaped the vultures in spite of its being the size of an ox kidney; but even then we did not dare believe in his death because it was the second time he had been found in that office, alone and dressed and dead seemingly of natural causes during his sleep, as had been announced a long time ago in the prophetic waters of soothsayers' basins.

Only his double had been able to show him his 'untruth': that useful ignoramus died of poison intended for his master. There had been a period when the President really was of the people, the easy joker who might easily get an upland bridegroom murdered so that he himself could possess the bride. The dictator's peasant mother who carried on in his mansion, sitting at her sewing machine as if she were still in her hut, was the only one aware of his tragedy. (Once when he was driving to a ceremonial parade she rushed after him with a basket of empties telling him to drop them at the shop when he passed. The violent book has many homely touches.) His brutal sexual assaults are not resented:—he fucks with his boots and uniform on—but when very late he comes to feel love, he is at a loss. On a Beauty Queen of the slum called the Dog District, he pours gadgets and imported rubbish, even turns the neighbourhood into a smart suburb: she is immovable and he is almost mad.

He kidnaps a Jamaican novice nun and marries her, but two years pass before he dares go to bed with her. She spends her time bargaining for cheap toys in the market. She surrenders to him not out of love but out of pity and teaches him to read and sign his name. The market people hate her trading habits and her fox furs and set dogs on her and her children: they are torn to pieces and eaten. There is a frightful scene where his supposedly loyal Minister organizes an insurrection. The old man's animal instinct detects a plot in the conspiracy. The Minister warns him: 'So things are in no shape for licking your fingers, general Sir, now we really are fucked up.' The wily President won't budge but sends down a cartload of milk for the rebels and when the orderly uncorks the first barrel there is a roar and they see the man

> floating on the ephemeral backwash of a dazzling explosion and they saw nothing else until the end of time in the volcanic heat of the mournful yellow mortar building in which no flower ever grew, whose ruins remained suspended in the air from the tremendous explosion of six barrels of dynamite. That's that, he sighed in the Presidential palace, shaken by the seismic wind that blew down four more houses around the barracks and broke the wedding crystal in cupboards all the way to the outskirts of the city.

The President turns to his dominoes and when he sees the double five turn up, he guesses that the traitor behind the rebellion is his old friend of a lifetime, the Minister. He is invited to a banquet and, at the stroke of twelve, 'the distinguished Mayor General Roderigo de Aguilar entered on a silver tray, stretched out, garnished with cauliflower and laurel, steeped with spices and oven brown—and, in all his medals, is served up roast.' The guests are forced to eat him.

Márquez is the master of a spoken prose that passes unmoved from scenes of animal disgust and horror to the lyrical evocation, opening up vistas of imagined or real sights which may be gentle or barbarous. The portrait of the mother who eventually dies of a terrible cancer is extraordinary. He has tried to get the Papal Nuncio to canonize her and, when Rome refuses, the President makes her a civil saint and has her embalmed body carried round the country. Avidly the people make up miracles for her. Once more, in his extreme old age and feeble, there is another insurrection, plotted by a smooth aristocratic adviser. The president survives. In his last night alive he wanders round the ruined house, counting his cows, searching for lost ones in rooms and closets; and he has learned that because of his incapacity for love he has tried to 'compensate for that infamous fate with the burning cultivation of the solitary vice of power' which is a fiction. 'We (the multiple narrator concludes less tritely) knew who we were while he was left never knowing it for ever . . .' The 'All' is not an extent, it is a depth.

Medallions

IN ONE OF his terse utterances about himself as an artist, Jorge Luis Borges says, 'I have always come to life after coming to books.' In a general sense this could be said by most storytellers and poets, but in Borges the words have a peculiar overtone. He appears to speak of something anomalous with the dignity of one who has been marked by an honourable wound received in an ambush between literature and life. Like Cervantes, he would have preferred to be a soldier who had pride in his wounded arm and had been forced by singularity into turning to the conceits of the *Exemplary Novels* and the *Romances* out of which he made *Don Quixote*.

Among South American writers Borges is a collection of anomalies, exceptional in the first place in having been brought up on English rather than French models; towards the Spaniards outside of *Don Quixote* (English translation preferred) and Quevedo, he is condescending. He had an English grandmother and an Anglophile father who was himself a writer and who brought up his son on *Tom Brown's Schooldays*, Kipling, Wells, Stevenson, Chesterton and Emerson. The poetry of Swinburne, Tennyson and Browning was important in the Argentine family who, on the Spanish side, had been violently concerned in earlier generations in the savage South American civil wars. The boy was frail and too near-sighted to follow a military career. Father and son, both slowly going blind, went to Europe for cure and education, mainly in Geneva, Germany and Spain. They detested Paris and thought Madrid trivial. One would guess that the erudition of Browning and the abrupt images of his dramatic narratives, made the deepest impression, though one sees no trace of this in Borges's own poetry. Returning to Buenos Aires where at first he could hardly leave his house, he eventually became a librarian in a small municipal library (from which he was dismissed for political reasons at the time of Perón), and later the Director of the National Library itself.

Borges has also spoken of how, after the age of thirty, when he began to go blind, he has lived physically in a growing twilight in which the distinctions between visible reality, conjecture and an immense reading are blurred. He had to remember, and a memory, in which he is rarely at a loss for the exact words of a long poem, has become literary, and the library a printed yet metaphysical domain. It is not surprising that Berkeley and Schopenhauer are his philosophers, and no more than natural, to one so attached to English literature, that he should have read William Morris and De Quincey. In conversation with Borges one hears life emerging out of phrases and scenes from literature and this, one understands at once from his writing, is not a merely browsing habit of mind. The emergence is dramatic, a creative act, as new landscapes are imagined and populated.

Such a reader is a full man, too full for the novelist. He has said:

I have read but few novels and, in most cases, only a sense of duty has enabled me to find my way to the last page. At the same time, I have always been a reader and re-reader of short stories—Stevenson, Kipling, Henry James, Conrad, Poe, Chesterton, the tales in Lane's translation of *The Arabian Nights*, and certain stories of Hawthorne have been a habit of mine since I can remember. The feeling that the great novels like *Don Quixote* and *Huckleberry Finn* are virtually shapeless, reinforced my taste for the short story form whose indispensable elements are economy and a clearly stated beginning, middle and end.

This sounds conventional enough. But in the writer of short stories as in the poet, a distinctive voice, unlike all others, must arrest us; in Borges the voice is laconic, precise yet rapt and unnerving; it is relieved by the speculations of the essayist and the disconnecting currents of memory. Even in a banal paragraph each word will create the sudden suspense made by a small move in chess. In the story of *Emma Zung*, a woman is shown getting a letter which tells her that her father whom she has not seen for years, has committed suicide: I give the English translation in which the dry exactitude of the Spanish is weakened—but still it catches the effect he desires:

> Her first impression was of a weak feeling in her stomach and in her knees: then of blind guilt, of unreality, of coldness, of fear; then she wished that it were already the *next* day. Immediately afterwards she realised that the wish was futile because the death of her father was the only thing that had happened in the world and it would go on happening endlessly.

Why did 'she wish it were the next day'? Why would the death 'go on happening endlessly' in real life? Because she is intent on revenge. These phrases ring in the imagination like an alarm bell, and this alarm is at the heart of all Borges's writing. The endlessness, the timelessness of a precise human experience, is his constant subject. How to convey the sense of endlessness curtly—with a vividness that is, on the face of it, perfunctory—will again and again be his dramatic task.

Nearly all the stories of Borges, except the earliest ones, are either constructed conundrums or propositions. The early ones are trial glosses on the American gangster tale transferred to the low life of Buenos Aires. He moved on to the stories of the gaucho: he heard many of these from his grandmother. They begin deceptively as short, historical reminiscences and then, at the crisis, they burst into actuality out of the past; he is recovering a moment:

Any life, no matter how long and complex it may be, is made up of *a single moment*—the moment in which a man finds out, once and for all, who he is.

In his stories of the gauchos, their violence will strike us as meaningless until Borges says:

> the gauchos, without realising it, forged a religion—the hard and blind religion of courage—and this faith (like all others) has its ethic, its mythology and its martyrs . . . they discovered in their own way the age-old cult of the gods of iron—no mere form of vanity, but an awareness that God may be found in any man.

The task of the writer in each story—it is usually a fight—is to find the testing crisis of *machismo*, as if he were chiselling it all out in hard, unfeeling stone. He is very careful to keep the tone of landscape or street low—he even refers to 'insipid streets' —in order to heighten the violence. The test may not be heroic, but will contain a dismissive irony. In *The Dead Man* a swaggering tough has been boasting to an able but ageing gang-leader. The gangs are expert cattle stealers. To the young man's surprise the old leader of the gang lets him get the better of him and even sends him up-country in charge of the next job. The gang obey the new young leader admiringly: the young man has even had the impudence to take the old leader's girl. They obey and love the young man. Why? Because he is the supplanter and winner? Because they are naturally treacherous time-serving cowards? Or simply recklessly indifferent? None of these things. An ancient knowledge comes to them. They *love* the young man because he is virtually dead already. He must be loved for his moment. They are really waiting, with interest, for the time when the old leader will come up-country, take his rightful revenge and kill him.

Or again, in a superb tale *The Intruder*, there are two brothers. A girl servant looks after them. She becomes the mistress of one brother, but when he goes off on his work the other brother sleeps with her. Both brothers fear their jealousy, so in the end they put the girl in a brothel. This does not solve their problem, for both secretly visit her. What is to be done? The test of their love for each other has arrived. They take her off at night and kill her. Lust is dead and now their love for each other is secure. Or there is the tale of Cruz, a soldier with a savage career behind him, who has been sent off to capture an outlawed murderer. The outlaw is cornered by Cruz and his soldiers and fights back desperately. Borges writes:

> Cruz while he fought in the dark (while his body fought) began to understand. He understood that one destiny is no better than another, but that every man must obey what is within him. He understood that his shoulder braid and his uniform were now in his way. He understood that his real destiny was as a lone wolf, not a gregarious dog. He understood the other man was himself.

So he turns against his own men and fights beside the outlaw. This is the story of the semi-mythical hero of the gauchos, Martin Fierro.

Because of the influence of the cinema, most reports or stories of violence are so pictorial that they lack content or meaning. The camera brings them to our eyes, but does not settle them in our minds, nor in time. Borges avoided this trap by stratifying his tales in subtle layers of flat history, hearsay and metaphysical speculation: he is not afraid of trailing off into a short essay, ending with an appendix, for the more settled a violent subject looks, the more we can be misled, the more frightening the drama. It will not only be seen to be true, but will have the sadness and dignity of a truth that our memories have trodden away. History, in Borges, is never picturesque or romantic. It is the past event coming back like a blow in the face.

When we turn to the fantasies of the poet in Borges we find him first of all at play with spoof learning. In one of his best known works with the extraordinary title of *Tlön, Uqbar, Orbis Tertius*, the librarian puts on a learned, dry-as-dust air of research and slyly reveals how for generations a secret society of pedestrian scholars have slowly invented an imaginary planet, complete with civilization and language derived from a faked edition of the Encyclopaedia Britannica, so that the non-existent has become established. Or in another tale he pretends to have discovered how the Idea of Luck gradually became rooted in the thought of a Compañía—a religious Order—who since ancient times have been inventing luck, little by little, by trial and error, until it pervades life and may be life itself. What they were really documenting was the monotony of life.

A more serious preoccupation comes close to nightmare. Our imaginations may be housed in intellectual constructions. The labyrinth is one. Or we may be enacting feelings, scenes or events that simply belong to 'an endless series'—a favourite phrase—over which we have no control. A fatalistic symbol of time or memory is a corridor with two mirrors facing each other: the infinitely repeated reflections are symbols of our consciousness of people, sensations and even things. Indeed things—a knife, a room, for example, and facts of landscape, having a threatening existence of their own and the dead force of inventory. In the story called *The Aleph* which contains his characteristic changes of voice, the narrator talks flatly of the death of a shallow society woman whom he had vainly loved:

On the burning February morning Beatriz Viterbo died after an agony that never for one single moment gave way to self-pity or fear, I noticed that the billboards on the sidewalk round Constitution Plaza were advertising some new brand of American cigarette. The fact pained me for I realised that the wide, ceaseless universe was already slipping away from her and that this slight change was the first of an endless series.

The narrator who is a poet heightens his pain by going to visit another poet, a boring man called Carlos Argentino Daneri who was a cousin of Beatriz and probably her lover. Daneri is

> authoritarian and unimpressive. His mental activity was continuous, deeply felt, far-ranging and—all in all—meaningless.

Daneri is writing an enormous poem which will conscientiously describe 'modern man' and everything on modern man's earth. The attack on realism and fact fetishism is obvious:

> Daneri had in mind to set to verse the entire face of the planet, and by 1941, had already despatched a number of acres of the State Queensland, nearly a mile of the course run by the River Ob, a gasworks to the north of Vera Cruz, the leading shops in the Conception quarter of Buenos Aires, the villa of Mariana Cambaceres de Alvear in the Belgrano section of the Argentine capital, and a Turkish baths establishment not far from the well known Brighton Aquarium.

In this curtly sarcastic comedy of jealousy over the grave of Beatriz Viterbo, Borges is leading us by the nose. He is preparing us for one of his eloquent imaginative leaps out of the dead world of things into a rhapsody on the tragedy of human loss. Daneri is annoyed that the narrator does not praise his poem and, knowing his man, says that embedded in the stairs of his cellar he possesses a great wonder which has inspired him and which will vanish tomorrow because the house is going to be pulled down. The wonder is a magic stone called the Aleph. The Aleph is the microcosm of the alchemists and Kabbalists, 'our true proverbial friend' (he calls it) 'the multum in parvo':

> Go down into the cellar, you can babble with all Beatriz Viterbo's images.

The narrator is locked in the cellar. He sees the stone which is only an inch wide:

In tha. single gigantic instance I saw millions of acts both delightful and awful; not one of them amazed me more than the fact that all of them occupied the same point in space, without overlapping or transparency. . . . I saw, close up, unending eyes watching themselves in me as in a mirror; I saw all the mirrors on earth and none of them reflected me; I saw in a backyard of Soler Street the same titles that thirty years before I'd seen in the entrance of a house in Fray Bentos; I saw bunches of grapes, snow, tobacco, lodes of metal, steam; I saw convex equatorial deserts and each one of their grains of sand; I saw a woman in Inverness whom I shall never forget; I saw her tangled hair, her tall figure; I saw the cancer in her breast; I saw a ring of baked mud in a sidewalk, where before there had been a tree. . . . I saw in a closet in Alkmaar a terrestrial globe betweeen two mirrors that multiplied it endlessly. . . . I saw in the drawer of a writing table (and the handwriting made me tremble) unbelievable, obscene, detailed letters, which Beatriz had written to Carlos Argentino; I saw the circulation of my own dark blood; I saw the coupling of love and the modification of death. . . .

The story ends in what is a typical Borges manner. There is a short discussion of the metaphysical theories about the Aleph which contains the malicious phrase 'Incredible as it may seem, I believe that the Aleph of Garay Street was a false Aleph'.

Our minds are porous and forgetfulness seaps in. I myself am distorting and losing, under the wearing away of the years, the face of Beatriz Viterbo.

In the story the shock of jealousy, grief and loss is transposed into a reel of mechanical effects.

In the elaborate fable of *The Circular Ruins*, a grey and silent teacher takes refuge in a ruined temple. 'His guiding purpose, though it was supernatural, was not impossible. He wanted to dream a man; he wanted to dream him down to the last detail and project him into the world of reality.' He 'creates' this phantom, thinks of him as his son; and then remembers that Fire is the only creature in the world who would know he was a phantom. In the end Fire destroys the dreamer. What is the meaning of the fable? Is it a fable of the act of creation in art? A solipsist conceit? A missing chapter from the Book of Genesis? An experience of panic caused by insomnia or reading Berkeley? Borges says,

> With relief, with humiliation, with terror, he understood that he too was a mere appearance dreamt by another.

One can argue that the later Borges is a learned pillager of metaphysical arguments: one who has made Chesterton rhapsodic, put blood into the diagrams of Euclid, or a knife into the hands of Schopenhauer, but the test of the artist is—Can he make his idea walk, can he place it in a street, a room, can he 'plant' the aftermath of the 'moment of truth'? Borges *does* pass this test. The poet is a master of the quotidian, of conveying a whole history in two or three lines that point to an exact past drama and intensify a future one.

To go back to the tale of Emma Zung. We see her preparing to avenge her father's death. To kill is a degrading act; first of all, therefore, she has to initiate herself into degradation by posing as a prostitute and sleeping with a sailor. She tears up the money he leaves her because to destroy money is impiety.

> Emma was able to leave without anyone seeing her; at the corner she got on a Lacroze streetcar heading west. She selected, in keeping with her plan, the seat farthest toward the front so that her face would not be seen. Perhaps it comforted her to verify in the insipid movement along the streets that what had happened had not contaminated things.

A small fact creates the impression of a link with some powerful surrounding emotion or some message from the imagination or myth. The very casualness of the sudden observation suggests the uncertainty by which our passions are surrounded.

Borges loves to borrow from other writers, either good or second-rate. He admires Poe who defined for all time what a short story intrinsically is. He certainly has been influenced by Kafka—he translated *The Castle* into Spanish—although he is far from being a social moralist. On the face of it he looks like one of the European cosmopolitans of the first thirty years of this century and, like them, very much a formalist. But on second thoughts one sees that his mind is not in the least European. The preoccupation with isolation, instant violence and the metaphysical journey of discovery or the quest for imagined treasure, marks him as belonging to the American continents. His sadness is the colonial sadness, not the European.

A bookish comment occurs to me. A few years ago when I was reading Borges for the first time I read two of the very late stories of Prosper Mérimée: *Lokis* and *La Vénus d'Ille*. There is a vast difference between the French Romantic and Borges, but they have one or two singular things in common. A short story writer cannot help being struck by the similarities that, in the course of more than 100 years, have diverged. Both writers have the English coolness and *humeur*, the background of the linguistic, historical, archaeological and mystical erudition. Mérimée was very much the wounded man, cold and detached, conservative and rational, but he had the civilized Romantic's fascination with the primitive and the unbelievable. In these two late stories—possibly because of a personal crisis—he is suddenly concerned with dream and the unconscious. It is true that the polished and formal Mérimée plays with his metaphysical anxieties, and has no interest in the self-creating man or woman, but he shares with Borges a love of hoaxing pedantry and the common approach of the misleading essay. The terrible story *Lokis* affects to arise in the course of a serious study of the Lithuanian language. (Mérimée was a philologist, so is Borges.)

Mérimée uses his learning to play down his subject for it will suddenly become a fantastic dream of the unconscious turned into gruesome reality. The same may be said of Mérimée's tale of Corsican vendetta and in the ghost story of *La Vénus d'Ille*.

A hundred and thirty years separate Mérimée and Borges. Where Mérimée's documentation is a closed study of folklore or custom, Borges takes a leap into space, into the uncertain, the mysterious and the cunning. The record has become memory feeding on memory, myth feeding on myth. Where Mérimée is the master of anecdote in which lives end when the artist decides, Borges has the poet's power to burst the anecdote open. He seems to say that the story must be open, because I, too, am like my characters, part of an endless series or repetitions of the same happenings. The risk is—and there are some signs of this already—that criticism of Borges will become an accretion that will force us to see his stories as conceits alone.

List of Books

List of Books

Books referred to

BORIS PASTERNAK

An Essay in Autobiography. Introduction by Edward Crankshaw. Translated by Manya Harari, 1959.
Prose and Poems. Edited by Stefan Schimanski. Introduction by J. M. Cohen. Translated by Beatrice Scott, Robert Payne, and J. M. Cohen, 1959.
Dr Zhivago. Translated by Max Hayward and Manya Harari, 1958.

ALEXANDER SOLZHENITSYN

August 1914. Translated by Michael Glenny, 1972.
Lenin in Zurich. Translated by H. T. Willetts, 1976.
First Circle. Translated by Thomas P. Whitney, 1968.
Cancer Ward. Translated by N. Bethell and D. Burg, 1968.
One Day in the Life of Ivan Denisovich. Translated by Max Hayward and Ronald Hingley, 1963.

ANTON CHEKHOV

The Letters of Anton Chekhov. Translated and edited by Avrahm Yarmolinsky with the assistance of Babette Deutsch, 1973.
The Letters of Anton Chekhov. Selected and edited by Simon Karlinsky. Translated by Michael Henry Heim in collaboration with Simon Karlinsky, 1973.
The Peasants. Translated by Ronald Hingley, 1965.
Eleven Stories. The Oxford Chekhov, 1950.
Life of Chekhov. By Ernest Simmons, 1950 and 1963.
Chekhov: The Evolution of his Art. By Donald Rayfield, 1975.
Anton Chekhov: A Life. By David Magarshack, 1953.

LEO TOLSTOY

Tolstoy. By Henri Troyat, 1968.
Russian Thinkers. By Isaiah Berlin, 1978.

IVAN GONCHAROV

Oblomov and his Creator: The Life and Art of Ivan Goncharov. By Milton Ehre, 1974.

FYODOR DOSTOEVSKY

Dostoevsky: The Seeds of Revolt, 1821–1849. By Joseph Frank, 1977.
Problems of Dostoevsky's Poetics. By Mikhail Bakhtin. Translated by R. W. Rotsel, 1973.
Dostoevsky and his Devils. By Václav Černý. Translated by F. W. Galan, with an afterword by Josef Skvorecky, 1975.
A Self-Portrait. Edited by Jessie Coulson, 1976.
The Undiscovered Dostoevsky. By Ronald Hingley, 1975.
Dostoevsky. By Konstantin Mochulsky. Translated by Michae Minihan, 1968.

ALEXANDER PUSHKIN

The Letters of Alexander Pushkin. 3 vols. Translated by J. Thomas Shaw, 1963.
Pushkin on Literature. Translated and edited by Tatiana Wolff, 1971.
Pushkin: A Comparative Commentary. By John Bayley, 1971.
Eugene Onegin. Translated by Charles Johnston, 1977.

AUGUST STRINDBERG

Getting Married. Translated and edited with an introduction by Mary Sandbach, 1972.

FRANZ KAFKA

Letters to Friends, Family and Editors. Translated by Richard and Clara Winston, 1978.

JEAN GENET

Funeral Rites. Translated by Bernard Frechtman, 1973.
The Vision of Jean Genet. By Richard N. Coe, 1968.

EMILE ZOLA

The Life and Times of Emile Zola. By F. W. J. Hemmings, 1977.

GEORGE SAND

George Sand: A Biography. By Curtis Cate, 1975.
Mauprat. With an introduction by Diane Johnson, 1978.
Lélia. Translated and with an introduction by Maria Espinosa, 1978.
The Companion of the Tour of France. Translated by Francis George Shaw, 1976.
The Haunted Pool. Translated by Frank Hunter Potter, 1976.

GUSTAVE FLAUBERT

The Novels of Flaubert: A Study of Themes and Techniques. By Victor Brombert, 1967.
Intimate Notebook 1840–1841. Translated by Francis Steegmuller, 1967.
The Dictionary of Accepted Ideas. Translated by Jacques Barzun, 1968.
November. Translated by Frank Jellinek. Edited by Francis Steegmuller, 1967.

STENDHAL

Stendhal: Fiction and the Themes of Freedom. By Victor Brombert, 1968.
Stendhal: Notes on a Novelist. By Robert M. Adams, 1968.
The Novel of Worldliness. By Peter Brooke, 1970.
Stendhal. By Joanna Richardson, 1975.

EÇA DE QUEIROZ

The Mandarin and Other Stories. Translated by Richard Franko Goldman, 1966.

The City and the Mountains. Translated by Roy Campbell, 1967.
The Illustrious House of Ramires. Translated by Ann Stevens, 1968.

BENITO PEREZ GALDOS

La de Bringas. Translated by Gamel Woolsey, 1951.
Fortunata and Jacinta: Two Stories of Married Women. Translated by Lester Clark, 1973.

MACHADO DE ASSIS

The Psychiatrist. Translated by William Grossman and Helen Caldwell, 1963.
Epitaph for a Small Winner. Translated by William L. Grossman, 1953 & 1968.
Dom Casmurro. Translated by Helen Caldwell, 1966.
Esau and Jacob. Translated by Helen Caldwell, 1966.

GABRIEL GARCIA MARQUEZ

The Autumn of the Patriarch. Translated by Gregory Rabassa, 1977.
One Hundred Years of Solitude. Translated by Gregory Rabassa, 1970.
Leaf Storm and Other Stories. Translated by Gregory Rabassa, 1973.

JORGE LUIS BORGES

The Aleph and Other Stories. 1933–1969. Translated by Norman Thomas Giovanni, 1971.
Labyrinths. Edited by Donald A. Yates and James E. Irby, 1961.

About the Author

V.S. PRITCHETT was born in 1900. In addition to being a critic, he is a short-story writer, novelist, biographer, autobiographer, and travel writer. Sir Victor is a foreign honorary member of the American Academy of Arts and Letters and of the Academy of Arts and Sciences. In 1975 he received a knighthood. He lives in London with his wife.